BORDEAUX & the PYRÉNÉES

A BICYCLE YOUR FRANCE GUIDEBOOK

Walter Judson Moore

Photographs, Maps and Graphics

by the Author

BORDEAUX & the PYRÉNÉES

A BICYCLE YOUR FRANCE GUIDEBOOK

ISBN-13: 978-1491271780

ISBN-10: 1491271787

A Walter Judson Moore imprint.

PO Box 490, Inverness

Florida 34451-0490 USA

wjmoore@tampabay.rr.com

On demand printing and distribution is by CreateSpace.com and their affiliate industries, its retail and online bookstore customers.

Print & Kindle® available at http://www.amazon.com/Walter-Judson-Moore/e/B003XWAFBG/ref=sr_tc_2_0?qid=1375176632&sr=1-2-ent

Adobe® Digital Editions for Apple® iPad® available at http:itunes.apple.com/us

Also by Walter Judson Moore:

BORDEAUX & the PYRÉNÉES QUEUE SHEETS

BURGUNDY EXPLORATIONS: A BICYCLE YOUR FRANCE GUIDEBOOK

BURGUNDY EXPLORATIONS QUEUE SHEETS

ROMAN PROVENCE & RHÔNE ALPES: A BICYCLE YOUR FRANCE GUIDEBOOK

ROMAN PROVENCE & RHÔNE ALPES QUEUE SHEETS

PROVENCE – LUBERON & LAVENDER: A BICYCLE YOUR FRANCE GUIDEBOOK

PROVENCE – LUBERON & LAVENDER QUEUE SHEETS

LOT VINEYARDS TO TARN GORGES: A BICYCLE YOUR FRANCE GUIDEBOOK

LOT VINEYARDS TO TARN GORGES QUEUE SHEETS

DORDOGNE VALLEYS AND VILLAGES: A BICYCLE YOUR FRANCE GUIDEBOOK

DORDOGNE VALLEYS AND VILLAGES QUEUE SHEETS

BICYCLE YOUR FRANCE: SECRET BURGUNDY

BICYCLE YOUR FRANCE: SECRET BURGUNDY QUEUE SHEETS

WRITING & CRAFTING A TRAVEL GUIDEBOOK: INSIGHTS & CONSIDERATIONS

THE TITOV LETTERS: a Novel of Development, Drama, and Life in the New Russia

SYNTHETIC SOVIET: a Novel of Biological Intrigue and Family Survival in a Failing System

Interactive commentary on this and future guidebooks are at http://bicycleyourfranceweekends.wordpress.com and at http://bicycleyourfranceweekends.wordpress.com

Table of Contents

Section	Page

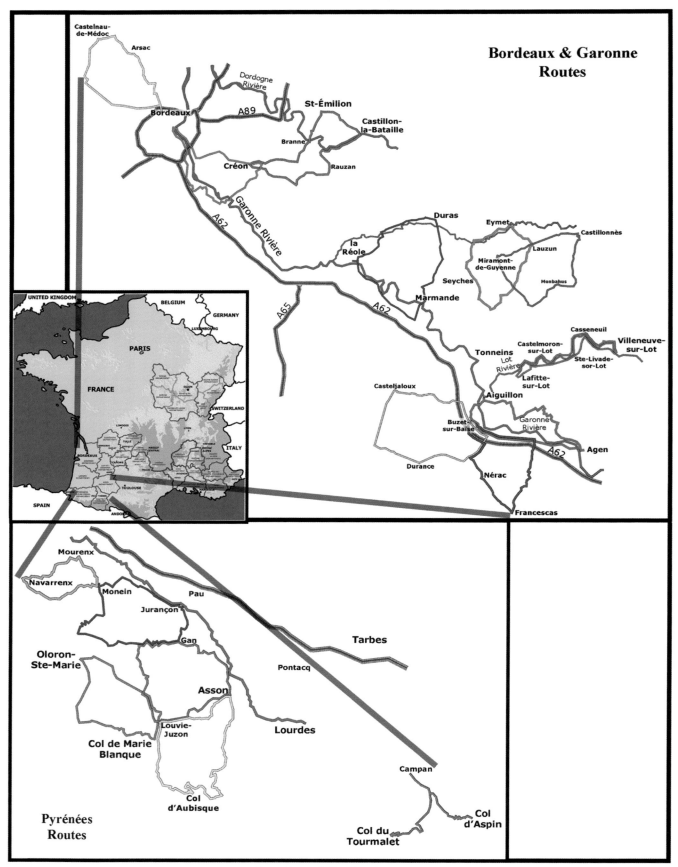

Bordeaux & Garonne Routes

Castelnau-de-Médoc
Arsac
Dordogne Rivière
St-Émilion
Bordeaux
A89
Castillon-la-Bataille
Branne
Créon
Rauzan
Garonne Rivière
A62
Duras
Eymet
Castillonnès
la Réole
Lauzun
Miramont-de-Guyenne
A65
Seyches
Monbahus
A62
Marmande
Casseneuil
Castelmoron-sur-Lot
Villeneuve-sur-Lot
Tonneins
Lot Rivière
Ste-Livade-sor-Lot
Lafitte-sur-Lot
Casteljaloux
Aiguillon
Buzet-sur-Baïse
Garonne Rivière
A62
Agen
Durance
Nérac
Francescas

UNITED KINGDOM
BELGIUM
GERMANY
LUXEMBOURG
PARIS
FRANCE
SWITZERLAND
LYON
ITALY
BORDEAUX
CAHORS
TOULOUSE
SPAIN
ANDORRA

Pyrénées Routes

Mourenx
Navarrenx
Monein
Pau
Jurançon
Tarbes
Gan
Oloron-Ste-Marie
Pontacq
Asson
Louvie-Juzon
Lourdes
Col de Marie Blanque
Campan
Col d'Aubisque
Col d'Aspin
Col du Tourmalet

Location of the Routes

1   Prolog

You can handle any and all of these sixteen routes, from the highest paved road in the Pyrénées to the flat woods in the Médoc. It all depends on your lungs, thighs, patience and proper selection of grandparents.

All the routes are through the Aquitaine Region of southwest France with its extraordinary history. The jagged, snow-capped peaks of the Pyrénées are breathtaking, physically and emotionally.

Col du Tourmalet Approach

Bordeaux wines, both the first growth and table wine, are as fine a value as they have been in decades. Most cyclists have an awareness of wines from the Médoc and St-Émilion, where there are routes. There are also routes through Entre deux Mers and Jurançon vineyards.

In addition to the routes way up four mountain passes, two routes utilize the Piste Cyclable Roger Lapébie, and four routes follow the cycle path along the Canal de Garonne.

Visit Eleanor of Aquitaine's city of Bordeaux, King Henry IV's château in Nérac, ask about Richard the Lionheart's chamber overlooking the Eymet central square, and walk around where the last battle of the Wars of Religion took place in Castillion-la-Bataille. Then throw in Castillonnès, Agen, Villeneuve-sur-Lot, Pau and Oloron-Ste-Marie. This becomes a journey through the Middle Ages.

Place des Arcades in Eymet

I often explain to a curious person that I recommend centering a cycling adventure in a single community for five to seven days. Should you rent a *gîte* (vacation cottage) near a selected village for a week, then bicycling from there in the morning and returning that afternoon clarifies some of this proposition. Since gîtes have kitchens, you may eat a breakfast necessary for moderate exercise. At the end of a day's ride, you may want to unwind with a beverage and just anticipate the evening's activity. That may include staying put, snacking, checking out a local restaurant and its cuisine, talking with the gîte's proprietor or photographing the local sheep and goats. Whatever your choice, you will recharge your spirit.

Entre Deux Mers Vineyard

Why this area of southwestern France? Well, perhaps it is to bike a few kilometers of a Tour de France out-of-category climb. It is not to follow the route of a Tour de France sprint stage on a road with heavy traffic. Only on the day of the Tour is traffic absent.

For the most part, motorists have not changed in rural France. They are still unexpectedly considerate toward cyclists. You can always stop beside the narrow, paved roads on these routes for a break and not be concerned by traffic. You may buy fresh produce from the farmer, a bottle of wine at a vineyard or pâté foie gras or real Spanish Paella in a morning market. How about riding 539 meters across the 164-year-old Pont du Garonne that carries the canal across the river to Agen — better yet, walk your bike. The length of the list is extensive. For certain, you will want to return.

Lévignac-de-Guyenne Sunday Market

Necessary details for travel to southwestern France are in this guide so that you arrive unruffled — well, at least not too agitated. Basic data are included on selecting a community, finding and renting a gîte, bringing your bike or renting a good one, having or renting a vehicle, driving in France, what to bring, buying groceries and something on restaurants.

There are sixteen cycling routes mapped and profiled (some may count the Col du Tourmalet and Col d'Aspin route as two). Each itinerary discusses a few villages and points of interest along the route. All circuits are on paved roads. Motor vehicle traffic on these routes is light, but riding single file is encouraged. One route does go into a real city, Bordeaux.

2   Preparation

When to Travel

Anytime during the year except early spring and winter will provide weather that is practical for cycling in southwestern France, although snow may block some high passes through May. My experience is that some months are more enjoyable than others.

This choice, along with the type and location of lodging, should narrow your planning decisions.

The area has mostly sunny and reasonably dry conditions with moderate temperatures in late May, June, September and October. The higher elevations are cooler at any time. In July and August the wine regions are full of vacationers.

Bordeaux Across Garonne Rivière in May

Lodging Categories

Accommodations are the next choice. There are four types of lodging to consider. First on my list for all eleven trips cycling in France have been gîtes for one or two weeks, starting on a Saturday afternoon. The routes listed in this guidebook are serviced by at least a thousand gîtes. Search for their locations and descriptions using Google, the Gîtes-de-France web site and at least a half dozen other sites.

Gîte la Vignotte South of Pau

These properties each have a listing with photos, and occasionally a review and rating. Typically these gîtes have two bedrooms with room for two people each, a kitchen/living room combination, a toilet room and a shower/washroom plus a place to store bikes and park cars. Prices are from €300 to €600 per week depending on the season, size, rating and location.

After staying in sixteen gîtes, I have found that they are clean, have everything assured in their online entry, plus knives, forks, spoons and cooking equipment.

It is my view that the gîte benefits that exceed price include having the choice to fix your own breakfast so you may start riding early with enough calories for the morning. Also, you might eat dinner at the gîte should you be weary at the end of a particular day. Living in a French village for a week, to paraphrase the credit card ad, may be priceless.

Try searching for a gîte's web site online. Less than half advertise and use the Gîtes-de-France service. Using a proprietor's web site may allow paying the deposit with PayPal or the XOOM service and paying the balance with Euros at the end of your stay. Quite often the gîte proprietor requires a €150 to €250 cash security deposit upon arrival. Check with the proprietor. Don't be surprised.

The French language paperwork from Gîtes-de-France is a bit of an annoyance, but after you translate it with an online site, you will understand that the contract is mostly for the benefit of the renter.

Sheets, pillowcases and bath towels are not normally included in the rental price but may be rented from the proprietor. The renter must take care of all cleaning or pay for it at the end. Water, gas for cooking and eight kilowatt-hours (enough for all applications except heating) per day are included in the price

Washer & Dryer in a Gîte: Exception to the Rule

Occasionally, a rather peculiar washing machine (it was designed in France; all the controls are in French) is available; ask for instructions at check in. A heavy wood or wire clothes dryer frame is usually in the gîte.

Most gîtes have exterior walls of half-meter thick stone. There are no air conditioners in southwestern France gîtes. Heating them is expensive. Bring an extra sweatshirt. There are plenty of blankets. If there is a fireplace, ask how much fuel wood costs.

The second popular accommodation choice is the *Chambre d'hôtes* (B&B).

Consider staying at a B&B for a day or more when you arrive, or longer. This should allow you to get used to the gentle pace of the area, and to let that piece of luggage, which escaped the notice of baggage handlers in Washington or Paris, catch up with you (it will get to you in about a day and the French Post will deliver it). Prices at B&Bs vary from €50 to €130 per night and include a continental breakfast.

A Chambre d'hôtes offering an evening *table d'hôte* (table of the hosts meal) can add a lot to the fun.

Sitting with others to enjoy a family style meal with exceptional cooking is an occasion you will remember. A typical price is €25 per person and includes an aperitif, three courses and local wine. European vacationers often prefer this venue as their evening meal. It becomes a wonderful way to meet people (your French language abilities may be tested).

In larger villages and towns, decent **Hotels** are available for €70 to €150 per night. The grand French **châteaux** offer exceptional luxury at grand prices. Their rates start at €300 per day, double occupancy, and can exceed €15,000 per day for the whole château.

Bon Viveur II Barge on the Canal de Garonne

A **canal barge** along the Canal de Garonne might be considered. It may have bicycles or allow you to bring the ones you rented.

Most villages and towns have **Campgrounds**. This seems to be the way many European vacationers spend their holidays. They camp in tents, caravans (travel trailers) and small motor homes. Utilities and outdoor grills are available; most have swimming pools, fishing areas and playgrounds. Prices seem to start at €15 per night.

Use the Internet to find hotels and campgrounds. You can try showing up, except in July and August, and hope for a space.

Lodging Location Selection

Selecting a location to center your cycling requires some thought. Starting each morning from a place near the Garonne Rivière near Buzet-sur-Baïse or close to Jurançon near Pau will benefit your lower torso at the end of a ride. Try to make a selection so you have a downhill return and a chance to grab a cold beverage fifteen minutes earlier at the gîte. It is also good to have restaurants and a supermarché fairly close.

You may cycle on six routes during a week from these villages. On most of the routes you can start right from the gîte, or drive up to 80 kilometers to begin cycling.

It is important to think about the distance between your last location and the departure airport, especially with an early morning flight schedule. The Google

Maps estimates of travel time between points A and B on regular roads is usually correct before 06:30.

Travel to Bordeaux

From North America, western Pacific countries and Europe, fly to Aéroport de Bordeaux-Mérignac (BOD). Valid passports are a must to get on any flight going to or coming from the European Union. Services from the airport into Bordeaux include Jet'Bus to the St-Jean train station, and bus line **1** to center city. Using a taxi to the center will cost between €20 and €30, and take about a half hour.

There are five daily trains from Paris Charles de Gaulle Airport to Bordeaux St-Jean station. The typical time is 4½ hours.

Driving time from London, UK, to Bordeaux via the Dover Channel Tunnel, is about eleven hours.

A most convenient way to get around the region is to rent a car at the airport.

Auto Rental

You have just arrived at Bordeaux-Mérignac and hauled your three bags and two carryon satchels off the baggage carrousel. Not a bad day: everything is accounted for. For purposes of this guide, you will be renting bicycles. Given two people with bicycles and luggage, the small Renault, four-door Kangoo van is a reasonable selection.

Kangoo & Bike

For one person with the necessary stuff for a couple weeks, a two-door Renault Bebop micro-van works, although fitting a bicycle with the front wheel installed may be a contest. Both the Kangoo and the Bebop are diesel-fueled, six-speed manual shift micro-vans that perform well even at the 130-kilometer/hour AutoRoute speed limits. Once you have a local map and your vehicle, load it, adjust the mirrors and seat, take a deep breath or two, and drive out of the parking lot.

Reasons to have a vehicle, in addition to hauling you and your stuff, include the requirement to pick up and return the bikes, and travel to the gîte. It is also useful for grocery shopping, traveling to routes that start a distance from the gîte, visits to châteaux and museums

on a bad weather day or after a ride, and the final return to commercial transportation.

Driving in France

Previous guides have included much of this information. Drive in France on the right side of the road. Everyone must wear a seatbelt. Don't talk or text on a cell phone while driving. The French rule *priorité à droite* grants the right-of-way to vehicles merging into 'your' lane and direction of travel (applies to bicycles), and is indicated by these signs.

priorité à droite **Signs**

The *rond points* (roundabouts or traffic circles) are of less concern now for drivers from the US, as it was ten years ago. Drivers inside the circle have the right-of-way over vehicles entering the circle.

rond points **Sign**

Vehicles must and do give cyclists at least 1½ meters clearance IF they are riding single file. Don't allow a car you are driving to come in contact with a bicycle; the law assumes the automobile driver to be at fault for any damages.

There is no right turn on a red traffic light unless there is a blinking green or yellow arrow. Best fuel prices are available at supermarchés. Fold in your side mirrors when you park close to traffic. A valid US or European Union drivers license works in France. Rental agencies want a license valid for six months from the time of the rental and that the driver is at least 25 years old. There are heavy fines and harsh penalties if you drink and drive. Don't do it.

Bicycle Rental

I do not fly my bike to France. I am not an aggressive cyclist with a multi-thousand dollar carbon fiber or titanium frame. I would suggest that you consider renting a bike that is like new and set up for cycling this hilly terrain.

Rental Bicycle

Renting a bicycle that is ready (except for mounting your saddle) when you pick it up and with the inner of three chain rings sized for steep hills costs between €110 and €125 per week (hybrid) to €180 (road bike). Carbon fiber frame road bikes and children's bikes are available. My source is O₂Cycles in Camblanes-et-Meynac located fourteen kilometers southeast of Bordeaux. The owner, Norbert Audouin, prefers to deliver your bicycles anywhere in and around Bordeaux.

What to Pack

Saddle, the one you sat on for miles/kilometers
Helmet
Bicycle computer that measures altitude and an extra battery
Flashing taillight
Compass, simple
Sunglasses
Riding gloves
Rearview mirror, eyeglass or helmet mounted
Allen wrench set, metric
Screwdrivers, small
Swiss Army knife
6" tie wraps
Shoelaces
Mosquito repellent
Sunscreen
First Aid Kit (fill a Ziploc plastic bag with items you know how to use)
Insect Bite Kit (a Ziploc plastic bag with one or two over-the-counter topical analgesics)
Cheap shower caps to cover your saddle and bike bag in case you duck into a café during a shower
Rack trunk-bag to hold all this stuff

Bicycle rentals include an air pump, a spare tube, a lock, handlebar bag with a map case, and a pannier rack. Toe clips always help while climbing and the rental shop may have simple ones.

Bicycles need to be secured in the back of a car so they don't damage the upholstery. Bungee cords work well. If you think you will need to take off the front tire to get the bike in a car, bring a pair of old tennis balls that are pierced and will fit over the front forks.

Pack the normal list of cycle wear for cool mornings and warmer afternoons. Include a rain jacket. Do pack High-Vis yellow outerwear to give autos and delivery trucks a chance to see you. Leg warmers are advisable, tires spit up stuff off the road. Should you want to visit a church you may wear loose fitting shorts.

Restaurants that are open for *déjeuner* (lunch) will seat cyclists as long as you are not late (which means arriving between 12:00 and 13:00).

For an evening meal at good restaurants, wear dress slacks, sport shirt or top, and casual shoes. A sport coat isn't necessary for men, but most people feel the need for a light jacket after dark.

Leave your cotton clothing home. They never seem to dry if they get damp. For evenings at the gîte bring a sweater or synthetic fleece or both.

Bring your digital camera with enough memory for 25 to 35 high-resolution images each day. Also bring extra batteries if your camera uses rechargeable ones. Of course, you will need a charger that works on 240-volt AC power (the model number label will list voltages allowed) and a plug converter for European outlets.

Euros and Credit Cards

For a bicycling holiday based from a gîte or chambre d'hôte, my experience leads me to estimate that you will spend between €120 and €150 per person per week in Euro currency plus the Euros for lodging paid at the end of your stay. It is unlikely that a chambre d'hôte will accept a credit card, and if you deal with the proprietor of a gîte directly, you can expect to pay cash.

Order some Euros from your local bank a few weeks before you travel. I found my bank's rate 7% less than the rates at U.S. and French airports.

Most restaurants and many cafés accept Master Card, Visa and American Express credit cards, although not appropriate for coffee or a few beers. Tips are always cash and not more than 5%, often in small change. Taxes and service are almost always included in the menu's price for an item.

Many waiters bring a credit card reader/printer to your table when you want to pay the bill with a credit card. The card is always in your sight.

You will pay with cash at the local *boulangerie-pâtisserie* (bakery). Petit Casino and Utile grocery stores in villages accept Master Card and Visa, as do *pharmacies* and *supermarché* chains.

You may use North American credit cards with the proper PIN to withdraw Euros at ATMs. You will pay a fee for the cash advance plus a foreign transaction fee. Contact the credit card company's 800 number before you travel. Tell them you will be using the card in France so they don't arbitrarily cut you off thinking someone stole your card number.

Only exchange U.S. dollars at a recommended exchange. No French banks make currency exchanges for people who do not have accounts. Ask at a hotel, if you are a guest, at the car rental agency or at the bicycle rental to recommend an exchange.

3   Route Ranking and Safety

The sixteen routes in the following sections are ranked on a challenge scale from 3.3 to 16.2 based on distance, climbing, estimated riding time, calories burned during the ride, the number of 200 meter ascents between 5% and 10%, and the number of 200 meter ascents over 10%.

The highest-ranking route of these is the Col du Tourmalet with a challenge rank of 16.2 (46.1 kilometers, 1,520 meters of climbing, 35 ascent segments over 10% and 43 ascent segments between 5% and 10%). On the other end of the scale for this guidebook is the Bordeaux & Médoc route with a challenge ranking of 3.3 (62.2 kilometers, 170 meters of climbing and no significant ascents).

The factors used to establish these rankings are all linear with the possible exception of calories. That simply suggests that the Col du Tourmalet route is about five times more strenuous than the Médoc route. I cycled these routes in 2013, and the relationship seems to hold (the Tourmalet is grueling).

I believe that all of these routes may be cycled and enjoyed by most competent and patient cyclists who ride two to four times a week. To increase the value and satisfaction of your vacation or holiday, increase your current cycling workout program as much as possible prior to your trip.

Plan to start a daily ride around 08:00 with a return around 16:30, making a midmorning café stop. Enjoy an hour and a half lunch (perhaps with wine), stopping for a number of photographs, gazing from an overlook, and waiting while other riders catch up.

Start the day with a complete breakfast. On these routes, the estimated energy needed is from 1,460 to 3,000 calories (156 pound male). Eat enough and don't get cranky. Snack during the ride. Drink enough liquid. Your body will tell you if you are trying too hard.

Experienced cyclists that ride close to motor vehicles know safety is the top priority. Also consider a few of the following items.

The last item to check before you start a ride is the route map, waypoints and a compass. Know which way to start out and where to make the first two or three turns.

Take a break from cycling when you feel tired, not alert or have taken an unplanned optional route.

If you step down, move off the roadway if possible.

Bordeaux Tram Tracks

Be careful crossing railroad and tram tracks, along with painted white roadway markings. If there is any dampness in the air, they are like wet glass. Those in Bordeaux are very treacherous, even when it is misting.

Be aware that with the extra weight of two bags, a bike becomes even more top-heavy than you may be used to. Tumbling into the ditch after a stop and leaving your bike on the road can be disturbing, especially for the delivery van following you. The driver won't laugh, but fellow cyclists may find such an incident entertaining after picking you out of the gully.

Do step down on steep ascents, but while you are still cycling find a less steep part of the hill, shift to a higher gear and then stop. You will have something to push against when you restart.

DO NOT speed downhill on a country lane into a turn. These roads are maintained using small loose gravel (chip seal) over sealing oil. For a couple days after this sort of maintenance, these surfaces have all the traction of Teflon. You might also have an inappropriate encounter with a pile of straw, a road full of goats or a flower market.

Lévignac-de-Guyenne Flower Market

Don't be so careful you miss the reason you are riding. On the other hand don't return to the starting point with dried blood on your new High-Vis yellow jersey.

Emergency telephone numbers from pay phones without a phone card or money:

SAMU (ambulance service).....................................**15**

Gendarmerie (police station) **17**

Pompier (fire station) **18**

All emergencies from a cell phone.......................**112**

4 Action List

The items cited need attention, and they all need consideration in parallel. This is a checklist of commitments and expenditures. Lodging, air travel and car rental may require non-refundable deposits and payments in full prior to travel. You should feel committed to the adventure when you pay the money.

- Select the approximate community locations that take advantage of cycling starting points.
- Decide when to travel.
- Select and reserve lodgings on-line.
- Buy airline tickets. Shop around. Airline web sites have equal or better fares than consolidators. Add baggage and other fees for a true comparison.
- Decide whether to take your own bicycle or to rent one. If you are renting, reserve it.
- Decide where you will need a vehicle, for how long and where to pick it up. Reserve a vehicle. Paying in advance with Europcar saves a percentage of the cost.
- If you will travel by train, decide on a schedule and buy the tickets, but no more than 60 days in advance. If you are bringing a bicycle, check that the particular train allows bikes.
- Decide what to take—A cell phone that works in Europe; Euros; credit cards; clothing; bike gear. Stage all the stuff and estimate the number of bags you need.

5 Queue Sheets Key and Map Symbols

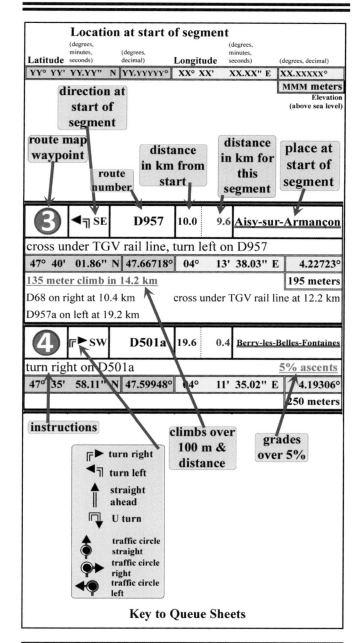

Key to Queue Sheets

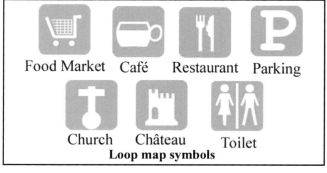

Food Market Café Restaurant Parking

Church Château Toilet

Loop map symbols

6 Bordeaux & the Médoc

Details:

Distance—62.2 kilometers

Climbing—170 meters

Challenge rank—3.3

Parking: Allée de Borges in Bruges, Bordeaux.

From Bruges, bicycle north 2½ kilometers to the *Piste Cyclable* (cycling track) Bordeaux Lacanau. Follow the Piste Cyclable 18½ kilometers west to Salaunes. From Salaunes, cycle north 11 kilometers to Castelnau-de-Médoc. Then ride east 3½ kilometers through Avensan and 7½ kilometers to Arsac. From Arsac the route heads generally south 18½ kilometers through the countryside back to Bruges.

The route has a few "bumps" but is rather easy going.

Piste Cyclable Bordeaux Lacanau

Cycle Path and Former Rail Line

Similar to many cycling paths in France, this one started out as a rail line. In the nineteenth century, the massive pines of the Landes forest were only accessible by one road and on a mule. To enable the transportation of wood and to improve the economy in 1871, the departmental government authorized construction of a railway and road improvements.

Salaunes

In 1881, a private railway developer bought a 99-year concession from the departmental authority. This

concession included a line from Bordeaux to Salaunes plus three other lines in the region.

The commissioning took place in 1885. At the line's opening, the stations included Bruges, St-Médard and Salaunes.

In 1884, the City Council of Lacanau decided to extend the line to Lacanau (opened in 1885) and to create a new resort on the coast.

Business was slow until 1913. Then World War I enabled the line to grow through 1934.

The transport of Germans and their equipment to the coast greatly increased traffic during World War II. From 1945, American diesel locomotives replaced steam locomotives. Then passengers disappeared in 1954; instead they drove to the beaches. The goods traffic, mostly made of wood, decreased in favor of the road and stopped completely in 1978 due to cash flow problems.

Today the only traces of this line are the passenger buildings, many converted to residences or a tourist office. The line has now been converted into a bike path.

Médoc

Certainly some fine wines of Bordeaux come from the Médoc. This area of the Gironde department has a strong local identity due to its particular history and its many components.

This is a true peninsula, bounded on the west by the Atlantic Ocean and on the east by the estuary of the Gironde Rivière. Its northern boundary is the mouth where the Gironde flows into the Atlantic Ocean. On the other hand, its southern boundary is somewhat arbitrary. This lower limit seems to be somewhere in the Bruges Swamp Nature Reserve.

The probable origin of the name is the Latin *in medio aquae* (between the waters).

There is little evidence of occupation by prehistoric people. Due to its climate and landscape, the Médoc offered only poor and flat terrain without caves or other shelters.

At the beginning of the Bronze Age (1,800 to 725 Before the Common Era), the Médoc showed its capabilities with all kinds of sculptures.

Vineyard Near Avensan

The Médoc was spared by the Gallic War and coexisted with the Bituriges Vivisques Celts. These Celts occupied the mouth of the Gironde Rivière with Bordeaux as their capital.

The Roman influence was profitable in the Médoc. It was during this period that the Romans introduced viticulture and the wine trade was born. Since that time, the Médoc is known through the world by its vineyards, from the most famous to merely typical.

Église St-Germain d'Arsac (1878)

Three main landscapes share the peninsula offering rich and contrasting environments. With its history, the Médoc now has some of the more famous vineyards in the world. These Bordeaux vineyards are located on the slopes of the Gironde. Also, the large pine forests produce wood and resin.

Officially attached to the Landes de Gascogne, these lands were originally swampy and unfit for cultivation and forestry. An 1857 law requires cultivation of the Landes de Gascogne. This law required municipalities of the Gironde department to drain a large part of the Médoc marshes thus creating forests. In these forests, a maritime pine grows that is used for its resin.

Castelnau-de-Médoc

The lordship of Castro Novo was created 1050. Roland de Castro Novo built Château de Castel-Nau in 1108 for use by several families until the fifteenth century. Then Sir Lord of Essenault d'Issan bought it. Also in 1108, the chapel Jacobi Castro Novo was built not far from the château. In the eighteenth century the chapel was fitted with a tower and later became Église St-Jacques. The château was destroyed in 1790 during The Revolution, and stones from the ruins were used to build a few houses near the city center.

Mairie of Castelnau-de- Médoc

(Waypoints continue on page 12)

Queues and Directions

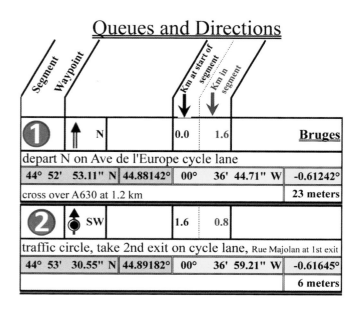

Segment	Waypoint		Km at start of segment	Km in segment	
①	↑ N		0.0	1.6	**Bruges**
depart N on Ave de l'Europe cycle lane					
44° 52' 53.11" N	44.88142°	00° 36' 44.71" W			-0.61242°
cross over A630 at 1.2 km					23 meters
②	⊙ SW		1.6	0.8	
traffic circle, take 2nd exit on cycle lane, Rue Majolan at 1st exit					
44° 53' 30.55" N	44.89182°	00° 36' 59.21" W			-0.61645°
					6 meters

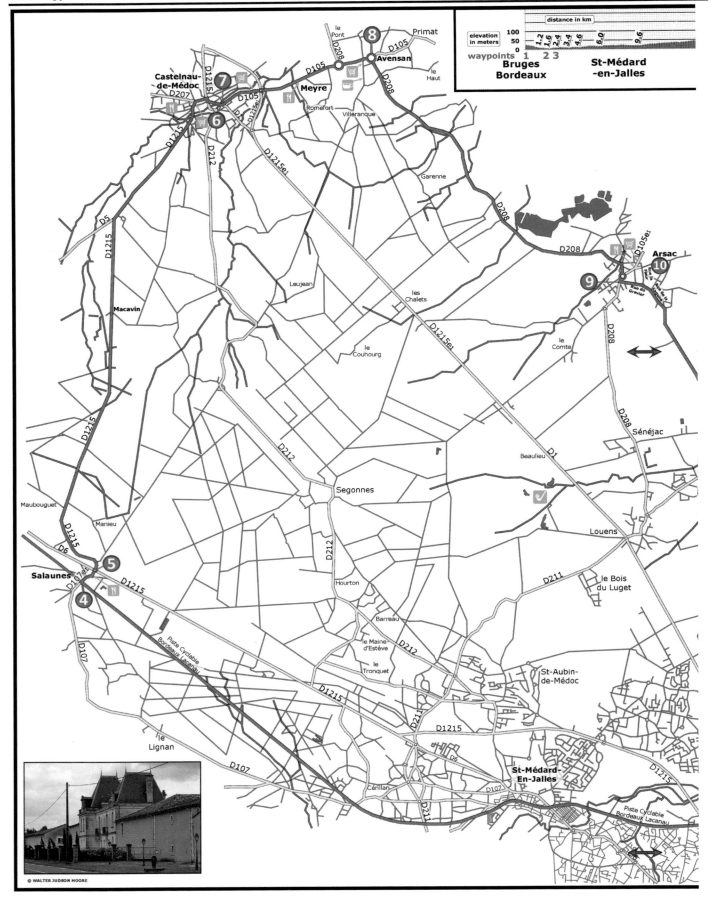

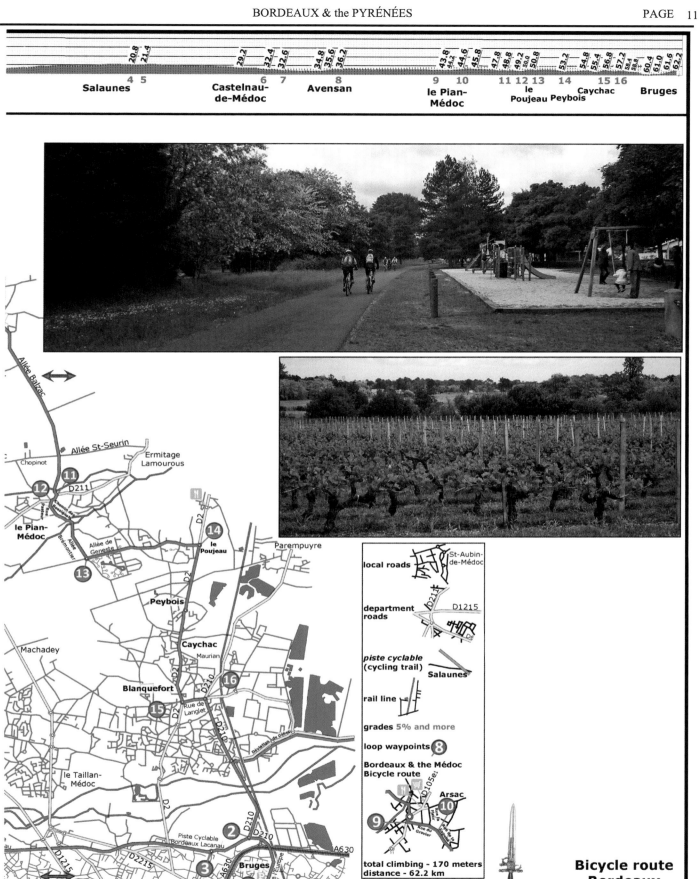

20.8	21.4		29.2	32.4	32.6	34.8	35.6	36.2		43.8	44.2	44.6	45.8		47.8	48.8	49.2	50.0	50.8		53.2	54.8	55.4	56.8	57.2	58.4	58.8	60.4	61.0	61.6	62.2

Salaunes 4 5   6 7 **Castelnau-de-Médoc** **Avensan** 8   9 10 **le Pian-Médoc** 11 12 13 14 **le Poujeau Peybois** 15 16 **Caychac** **Bruges**

local roads   St-Aubin-de-Médoc

department roads   D1215

piste cyclable (cycling trail)   Salaunes

rail line

grades 5% and more

loop waypoints (8)

Bordeaux & the Médoc Bicycle route
                                                    Arsac
(9)   (10)

total climbing - 170 meters
distance - 62.2 km

0   1   2 km

Bicycle route
Bordeaux
& the Médoc

3 ⊙►W | | 2.4 | 18.4 | |

traffic circle, take 1st exit on Piste Cyclable Bordeaux Lacanau

44° 53' 21.59" N	44.88933°	00°	37' 34.92" W	-0.62637°
cross D2 at 3.4 km		cross D2215 at 4.6 km		**7 meters**
cross under D1215 at 6.0 km		**St-Médard-en-Jalles** at 9.6 km		
cross D211 at 12.0 km		cross D107 at 13.6 km		

4 ┌►N | **D107e1** | 20.8 | 0.6 | **Salaunes**

turn right on D107e1

44° 56' 08.87" N	44.93580°	00°	49' 54.12" W	-0.83170°
				48 meters

5 ↕N | **D1215** | 21.4 | 11.0 | **Salaunes**

traffic circle, take 2nd exit on D1215, D1215 at 1st exit

44° 56' 16.05" N	44.93779°	00°	49' 40.31" W	-0.82786°
D5 on left at 29.2 km				**48 meters**

6 ┌►NE | **D207** | 32.4 | 0.2 | **Castelnau-de-Médoc**

turn right on D207

45° 01' 36.74" N	45.02687°	00°	48' 05.62" W	-0.80156°
				22 meters

7 ┌►E | **D105** | 32.6 | 3.6 | **Castelnau-de-Médoc**

turn right on D105

45° 01' 39.56" N	45.02766°	00°	47' 54.31" W	-0.79842°
traffic circle, take 2nd exit on D105, D1215e1 on 1st exit at 33.8 km				**21 meters**
Meyer at 34.8 km		traffic circle, take 1st exit on D105 at 35.6 km		

8 ⊙►SE | **D208** | 36.2 | 7.6 | **Avensan**

traffic circle, take 1st exit on D208

45° 02' 00.33" N	45.03343°	00°	45' 20.93" W	-0.75581°
				22 meters

9 ◄SE | | 43.8 | 0.8 | **Arsac**

turn left on Rue de Cazeau Vieil

44° 59' 37.19" N	44.99366°	00°	41' 36.09" W	-0.69336°
becomes Rue de Gravier at 44.2 km				**24 meters**

10 ┌►SE | | 44.6 | 4.2 | **Arsac**

turn right on Rue de la Lagune

44° 59' 31.44" N	44.99207°	00°	41' 05.71" W	-0.68492°
becomes Allée Balzac at 45.8 km		cross Allée St-Seurin at 47.8 km		**24 meters**

11 ┌►SW | **D211** | 48.8 | 0.4 | |

turn right on D211

44° 57' 26.91" N	44.95748°	00°	40' 06.30" W	-0.66842°
				23 meters

12 ◄S | | 49.2 | 1.6 | |

turn left on Rue Pasteur

44° 57' 22.48" N	44.95624°	00°	40' 21.52" W	-0.67264°
becomes Allée Brémontier at 50.0 km				**22 meters**

13 ◄⊙E | | 50.8 | 2.4 | |

traffic circle, take 3rd exit on Allée de Geneste

44° 56' 43.33" N	44.94537°	00°	39' 37.03" W	-0.66029°
le Poujeau at 52.8 km				**28 meters**

14 ⊙►S | **D2** | 53.2 | 3.6 | **le Poujeau**

traffic circle, take 1st exit on D2

44° 56' 53.52" N	44.94820°	00°	37' 51.21" W	-0.63089°
Peybois at 54.6 km				**15 meters**
traffic circle, take 2nd exit on D2				**Ceychac** at 55.4 km

15 ◄⊙E | | 56.8 | 0.4 | **Blanquefort**

traffic circle, take 3rd exit on Rue Jean Duvert

44° 55' 03.47" N	44.91763°	00°	38' 03.48" W	-0.63430°
becomes Rue de Langlet at 57.0 km				**24 meters**

16 ⊙►S | **D210** | 57.2 | 5.0 | |

traffic circle, take 1st exit on D210 cycle lane

44° 55' 05.50" N	44.91819°	00°	37' 43.29" W	-0.62869°
traffic circle, take exit on D210 cycle lane at 58.4 km				**18 meters**
traffic circle, cross D210 to cycle lane at 58.8 km		cross over A630 at 61.0 km		
traffic circle, take exit on D210 cycle lane at 60.4 km				
becomes Ave de l'Europe cycle lane at 61.6 km				

		62.2		parking, **Bruges**

Playground Along Piste Cyclable

7 Bordeaux, Créon & Langoiran

Details:

Distance—63.6 kilometers

Climbing—280 meters

Challenge rank—4.9

Parking: next to the Basilica of St-Michel in Bordeaux or in one of many lots along the Garonne Rivière.

Bicycle northeast across the Garonne Rivière and southeast along the river to Latresne. From Latresne, follow the Piste Cyclable Roger Lapébie 19 kilometers through Créon to la Sauve. After the turn at la Sauve, cycle southwest 12 kilometers to Langoiran. Bicycling north and west along the Garonne Rivière from Langoiran, follow the route 12½ kilometers back to Latresne. Then the route is on the Piste Cyclable to the Pont de Pierre and Bordeaux.

There is one slight climb on the route. It starts after the first crossing of the Garonne and climbs gradually 100 meters in 23.6 kilometers.

Bordeaux

This fair-sized city with a population of about a quarter million is the ninth largest city in France and is the capital of the Aquitaine region.

Place de la Victoire

Bordeaux is a major wine industry center. It is home to the world's main wine fair, Vinexpo. The wine economy in the metropolitan area is responsible for 14½ billion Euros annually. This trade started in the eighth century. The historic part of the city is on the UNESCO World Heritage List as "an outstanding urban and architectural ensemble" of the eighteenth century.

Around 300 Before the Common Era (BCE), Bordeaux was settled by the Bituriges Vivisques, a Celtic tribe. In 107 BCE, the Romans fought a conflict of the Gallic Wars called the Battle of Burdigala and lost to the Tigurini Celts.

The city finally fell to Roman rule around 60 BCE, its significance lying in exporting tin and lead to Rome. Later it became capital of Roman Aquitaine, flourishing during the third century. In 276 Common Era (CE) it was sacked by the Vandals. Further damage was caused by the same Vandals in 409 CE, the Visigoths in 414 CE and the Franks in 498 CE, thus beginning a period of obscurity for the city.

Cycle Lane Along Quai des Salinières

In the late sixth century, the city reappeared as the seat of a county and an archdiocese within the Merovingian kingdom of the Franks, although Frankish power was never strong. The city started to play a regional role as a major urban center on the fringes of the newly founded Frankish Duchy of Vasconia.

The city was plundered in 732, and again in 736. Sometimes the Counts of Bordeaux held the title alongside the Duke of Vasconia under the Carolingians. They were meant to keep in check the Basques and defend the mouth of the Garonne Rivière from the Vikings when the latter appeared in 844 around Bordeaux. In autumn 845, count Seguin II marched on the Vikings attacking Bordeaux but was captured and put to death.

From the twelfth to the fifteenth century, Bordeaux regained importance following the marriage of Duchess Eleanor of Aquitaine, her second of four, with the French-speaking Count Henri Plantagenet who became, within months of their wedding, King Henry II of England. The city flourished, primarily due to wine trade, and the cathedral of St. André was built. It was also the capital of an independent state under Edward, the Black Prince (1362–1372), but in the end, after the Battle of Castillon (1453), France annexed it.

In 1462, Bordeaux installed a parliament, but regained importance only in the sixteenth century when it became the center for the distribution of sugar and slaves from the West Indies along with the traditional wine.

Bordeaux adhered to the Fronde, one of two civil wars in France that ended the Thirty Years War. The city was effectively appropriated to the Kingdom of France only in 1653, when the army of Louis XIV entered the city.

Pont de Pierre

The eighteenth century was the golden age of Bordeaux. Many downtown buildings, including those along the river, are from this period. Victor Hugo found the town so beautiful he once said: "take Versailles, add Antwerp, and you have Bordeaux". Baron Haussmann, a long-time political figure in Bordeaux, used Bordeaux's eighteenth-century large-scale rebuilding as a model when he was asked by Emperor Napoleon III to transform a then still quasi-medieval Paris into a "modern" capital that would make France proud.

Porte de Bourgogne

In 1870, at the beginning of the Franco-Prussian war, the French government relocated to Bordeaux from Paris. This happened again during the First World War and again very briefly during the Second World War, when it became clear that Paris would soon fall into German hands. However, on the last of these occasions the French capital was soon moved again to Vichy.

From 1940 to 1943, the Italian Royal Navy established a submarine base at Bordeaux. Italian submarines participated in the Battle of the Atlantic from this base, which was also a major base for German U-boats.

The vine was introduced to the Bordeaux region by the Romans, probably in the first century, to provide wine for local consumption, and wine production has been continuous in the region since then.

Bordeaux now has about 116,160 hectares (287,000 acres) of vineyards, 57 appellations, 10,000 wine-producing châteaux and 13,000 grape growers. With an annual production of approximately 960 million bottles, Bordeaux produces large quantities of everyday wine as well as some of the most expensive wines in the world. Included among the latter are the area's five *premier cru* (first growth) red wines

Both red and white wines are produced in Bordeaux. Red Bordeaux is called claret in the United Kingdom.

Because of a glut in table wine production and the price squeeze by strong international competition, the number of growers has recently dropped from 14,000 and the area under vine cultivation has also decreased significantly. In the meanwhile, the global demand for the first growths and the most famous labels markedly increased and their prices have increased.

Located on the northern edge of Bordeaux, the Laser Mégajoule complex is developing one of the most powerful lasers in the world, allowing fundamental research and the elaboration of laser and plasma technologies.

20,000 people work in the Bordeaux aeronautics industry. The Dassault Falcon private jets are built here as well as the military's Rafale and Mirage 2000, the Airbus A380 cockpit and the boosters of Ariane 5 missile.

A Bordeaux Tram

The Bordeaux tramway network consists of three lines serving the city. The first line was opened on 21 December 2003, with additional extensions that increased the route length to 43.9 kilometers. The system is noteworthy for using a ground-level power supply of the Alimentation par Sol system in the city center.

No surprise, tourism, especially wine and cycling tourism, is a major industry.

Piste Cyclable Roger Lapébie

The Roger Lapébie (winner of the 1937 Tour de France while being the first contender to use a derailleur) bike path follows an old railway line between Latresne and Sauveterre-de-Guyenne. Starting late in 2009, a continuous cycle path connects Latresne to downtown Bordeaux. This greenway has an asphalt surface with well-marked intersections. In most sections the width is two meters.

Halfway through, the Créon station has water, toilets, parking, an area for motorhomes, a picnic area, information and a bicycle rental shop.

Piste Cyclable Roger Lapébie

This greenway begins in Bordeaux along the Garonne Rivière at Pont St-Jean, just a few hundred meters from the Stone Bridge and Place Stalingrad. From Latresne it is on the old railway line. Initially it follows the valley of the Pimpine along a shady and damp valley. Then it climbs a gentle slope for four kilometers to Créon.

After taking a lighted tunnel, it winds through the hills, through fields and woods, with regular ups and downs. In the final section, the greenway crosses vineyards and winds down to Sauveterre-de-Guyenne.

Créon

From 1152 and the marriage of Eleanor of Aquitaine to Henry Plantagenet, the Aquitaine was attached to the crown of England. In 1315, King Louis X, Duke of Aquitaine, who also was King Edward II of England, ruled France. In the Entre-deux-Mers (Between the Seas) area, King Edward II, was not challenged at first, but the Church was very influential. At the foot of the Abbaye de La Sauve, a community developed gradually and took business from the abbaye's shops. The abbaye collected taxes from all the people under its control: merchants paid various rights, such as tolls. All that money contributed greatly to the wealth of the abbaye. Edward II had no outpost in the forest of La Sauve, to the point that the king's provost needed to ask hospitality from the monks. The king did not even have a prison, which was his symbol of justice in Entre-deux-Mers. These then are the elements that led to establishing the fortified bastide of Créon. The bastide became subject to the founder, Edward II, who saw an increase in his political influence and economic power.

Place de la Prévoté

The establishment of a bastide raised from the Abbaye de La Sauve an immediate and long-term negative response. This intrusion on its territory was inconceivable and there remained a severe tension between the king and religious people. The provost marshal moved to Créon. In addition, the Benedictine influence declined with the introduction of a weekly Tuesday market at Créon in direct competition with the Benedictine's Tuesday market. A compromise agreement moved the Créon market to Wednesday. Until The Revolution, Créon was the seat of the Grand Provost Royal of the Entre-deux-Mers and had jurisdiction over 48 surrounding communities.

Since 1315, a market, with as many as a hundred traders and producers, takes place on Wednesdays.

Créon was the first Cycling in France station as part of the national pilot project in 1999. Bernard Hinault opened it on 23 July 2003. It developed along the former route of the railway connecting Latresne to Sauveterre-de-Guyenne and gradually became the Piste Cyclable Roger Lapébie.

The bastide uses an orthogonal grid around a central square. The plan is characteristic of bastides of the region. In the case of Créon, the choice of location was one of the crossroads between Bordeaux and Sauveterre. The intersection of the two sides formed the central square. The rest of the town had perpendicular streets and was surrounded by a rampart with fences, ditches, walls and four fortified entrance doors.

The single-nave church, as almost always in bastides, is close to the square. In Créon, building of the church started in 1316, and was completed in 1320. It is probably the foundation of the current church.

Because of the difficulties with the Abbaye of La Sauve, it was not until 1342 that Créon became a parish. Over the years the construction of the church continued to make it more consistent with the stature as the capital of the Entre-Deux-Mers.

(Continued on page 18)

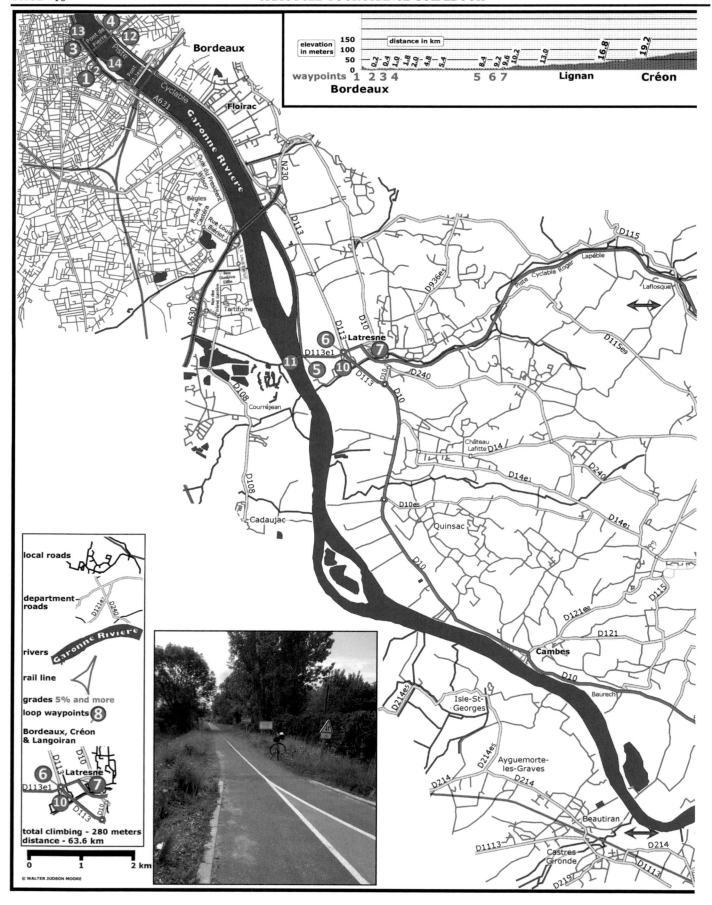

Bordeaux

Floirac

elevation
in meters

distance in km

waypoints

Bordeaux

Lignan

Créon

Garonne Riviere

Cyclable

A631

Quai du president Wilson

Bègles

R. des Castéra

Rue Louis Blériot

Rue Gustave Eiffel

Tartifume

Courréjean

Cadaujac

Latresne

D113e1

Château Lafitte

D14

Quinsac

Cambes

Isle-St-Georges

Ayguemorte-les-Graves

Beautiran

Castres Gironde

Legend

local roads

department roads

rivers — Garonne Riviere

rail line

grades 5% and more

loop waypoints

Bordeaux, Créon
& Langoiran

Latresne

D113e1

total climbing - 280 meters
distance - 63.6 km

0   1   2 km

© WALTER JUDSON MOORE

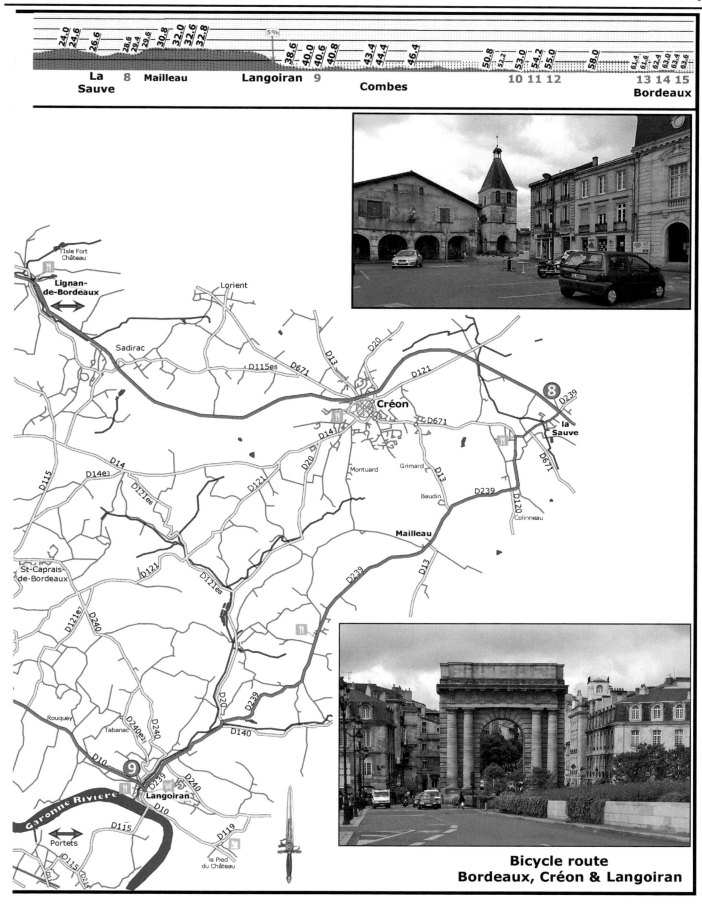

Profile markers: 24.0 24.6 26.6 | 28.6 29.4 29.6 30.8 32.0 32.6 32.8 | 5% | 38.6 40.0 40.6 40.8 43.4 44.4 46.4 | 50.8 52.2 53.0 54.2 55.0 | 58.0 | 61.4 61.6 62.4 63.0 63.4 63.6

La Sauve   8   Mailleau   Langoiran   9   Combes   10 11 12   13 14 15   Bordeaux

**Bicycle route
Bordeaux, Créon & Langoiran**

Until the late nineteenth century, burials were in the parish cemetery around, or inside, the church.

Arcades Around Place de la Prévoté

Houses that are decorated with arcades surround the central square, at 70 meters on a side. The dimensions are almost the same everywhere and are not related to the number of inhabitants. Additionally, four squares of the same size are at the corners of Créon.

The community hall opens onto the square in alignment with the houses. In Créon, the square is lined with arcades on three sides

Château du Langoiran

The Lords of Langoiran were one of the most prestigious and powerful elements of the Duchy of Aquitaine. They were involved in the struggle between the kings of England and France. Lords of Langoiran were all in the service of the Duke of Aquitaine, King of England, except Bérard d'Albret at the end of his life, after being captured by the constable of Eymet in 1374. He was forced to swear allegiance to the king of France.

Amanieu Albret, Lord of Langoiran was a lord of Biscay. On 3 July 1294, he was charged, along with Jean de Bretagne, Jean St-Jean and Robert Tybtot to arrange an alliance between the King of England and King of Castile. Edward I wrote to him on 19 October 1295, to thank him for his good offices. Some years later, on 6 November 1307, he was one of those who were appointed to negotiate the marriage of the King of England with Isabella, daughter of Philip the Fair and discuss the princess' dowry.

After the capitulation of Bordeaux in 1453, Charles VII of France demanded that twenty of the Gascon lords be turned over as hostages. Among them was Montferrand, the lord of Langoiran, who fled to England. The château was confiscated and entered the royal domain. It was given to Armagnac, Marshal of France. King Louis XI took in this area. As in other

areas after he had overturned the oppression policy of his father, he forgave Montferrand and restored to him a portion of their property of the Château du Langoiran.

During the Wars of Religion, the lordship of Langoiran passed successively into the hands of two rival brothers, Charles de Montferrand, leader of the Catholics in Bordeaux and Governor Guy Montferrand, one of the leaders of the party protesting for Guyenne. According to him, the family had to sell the castle Montferrand and the barony of Langoiran to the bourgeois, ennobled Arnold family.

To avenge the defeat of his troops, the Duke of Epernon, governor of Guyenne, seized the château in September 1649, blew up the dungeon and set the château on fire.

On 25 August 1944, elements of The Resistance column Druilhe camped at Langoiran. The next evening, at midnight, colonels Druilhe and Adeline (main leaders of The Resistance of Dordogne) agreed to the surrender of Bordeaux signed by Korvetten-Kapitän Ernst Kühnemann, which controlled the military port of Bordeaux starting in August 1941.

The château has a large dungeon built in the fourteenth century. The tower consisted of two floors connected by a vaulted staircase. The first floor was eight meters high up the keystone (which has been preserved and is located near the well) and was paved with tiles showing the arms of the lords of Escoussan.

Château du Langoiran

The vaults were painted and covered with a sprinkling of gold in the background and the coat of arms of the family. On all ribs of the arches were painted coats of arms of families who subsequently owned the property. On the ground floor is the guardroom equipped with a huge fireplace and a stone sink inside an arched cavity. On the first floor there are two frescoes dating from the construction of the tower, one representing St-Michael holding a balance in his left hand and a spear in the right. His head is haloed with waving hair. The devil, as usual, tries to tip the balance, but is foiled by the archangel.

Another mural depicts St-Peter who holds the keys of heaven. Over time, other frescoes adorning the walls in different vaults of the castle have disappeared. The second floor was the home of Lord and his family and his guests. This room was not vaulted. At this level, a large Gothic mullioned window was constructed in the late fourteenth century. An exceptional and rare gothic fireplace was placed inside a wall. In the sixteenth century, on the lower floor, a new chimney was built.

Queues and Directions

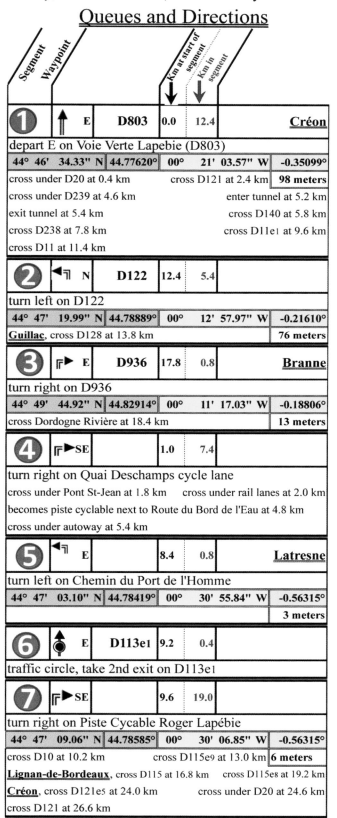

Column labels: Segment · Waypoint · Km at start of segment · Km in segment

1 ↑ E — D803 — 0.0 — 12.4 — **Créon**

depart E on Voie Verte Lapebie (D803)

44° 46' 34.33" N	44.77620°	00°	21' 03.57" W	-0.35099°

cross under D20 at 0.4 km	cross D121 at 2.4 km	98 meters
cross under D239 at 4.6 km	enter tunnel at 5.2 km	
exit tunnel at 5.4 km	cross D140 at 5.8 km	
cross D238 at 7.8 km	cross D11e1 at 9.6 km	
cross D11 at 11.4 km		

2 ◄⌐ N — D122 — 12.4 — 5.4

turn left on D122

44° 47' 19.99" N	44.78889°	00°	12' 57.97" W	-0.21610°

Guillac, cross D128 at 13.8 km	76 meters

3 ⌐► E — D936 — 17.8 — 0.8 — **Branne**

turn right on D936

44° 49' 44.92" N	44.82914°	00°	11' 17.03" W	-0.18806°

cross Dordogne Rivière at 18.4 km	13 meters

4 ⌐►SE — 1.0 — 7.4

turn right on Quai Deschamps cycle lane

cross under Pont St-Jean at 1.8 km	cross under rail lanes at 2.0 km
becomes piste cyclable next to Route du Bord de l'Eau at 4.8 km	
cross under autoway at 5.4 km	

5 ◄⌐ E — 8.4 — 0.8 — **Latresne**

turn left on Chemin du Port de l'Homme

44° 47' 03.10" N	44.78419°	00°	30' 55.84" W	-0.56315°
				3 meters

6 ⌾ E — D113e1 — 9.2 — 0.4

traffic circle, take 2nd exit on D113e1

7 ⌐►SE — 9.6 — 19.0

turn right on Piste Cycable Roger Lapébie

44° 47' 09.06" N	44.78585°	00°	30' 06.85" W	-0.56315°

cross D10 at 10.2 km	cross D115e9 at 13.0 km	6 meters
Lignan-de-Bordeaux, cross D115 at 16.8 km	cross D115e8 at 19.2 km	
Créon, cross D121e5 at 24.0 km	cross under D20 at 24.6 km	
cross D121 at 26.6 km		

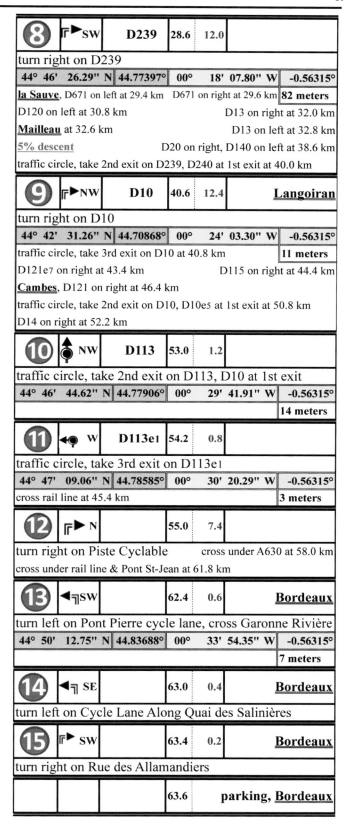

8 ⌐►SW — D239 — 28.6 — 12.0

turn right on D239

44° 46' 26.29" N	44.77397°	00°	18' 07.80" W	-0.56315°

la Sauve, D671 on left at 29.4 km	D671 on right at 29.6 km	82 meters
D120 on left at 30.8 km	D13 on right at 32.0 km	
Mailleau at 32.6 km	D13 on left at 32.8 km	
5% descent	D20 on right, D140 on left at 38.6 km	
traffic circle, take 2nd exit on D239, D240 at 1st exit at 40.0 km		

9 ⌐►NW — D10 — 40.6 — 12.4 — **Langoiran**

turn right on D10

44° 42' 31.26" N	44.70868°	00°	24' 03.30" W	-0.56315°

traffic circle, take 3rd exit on D10 at 40.8 km	11 meters
D121e7 on right at 43.4 km	D115 on right at 44.4 km
Cambes, D121 on right at 46.4 km	
traffic circle, take 2nd exit on D10, D10e5 at 1st exit at 50.8 km	
D14 on right at 52.2 km	

10 ⌾ NW — D113 — 53.0 — 1.2

traffic circle, take 2nd exit on D113, D10 at 1st exit

44° 46' 44.62" N	44.77906°	00°	29' 41.91" W	-0.56315°
				14 meters

11 ◄⌾ W — D113e1 — 54.2 — 0.8

traffic circle, take 3rd exit on D113e1

44° 47' 09.06" N	44.78585°	00°	30' 20.29" W	-0.56315°

cross rail line at 45.4 km	3 meters

12 ⌐► N — 55.0 — 7.4

turn right on Piste Cyclable	cross under A630 at 58.0 km
cross under rail line & Pont St-Jean at 61.8 km	

13 ◄⌐SW — 62.4 — 0.6 — **Bordeaux**

turn left on Pont Pierre cycle lane, cross Garonne Rivière

44° 50' 12.75" N	44.83688°	00°	33' 54.35" W	-0.56315°
				7 meters

14 ◄⌐ SE — 63.0 — 0.4 — **Bordeaux**

turn left on Cycle Lane Along Quai des Salinières

15 ⌐► SW — 63.4 — 0.2 — **Bordeaux**

turn right on Rue des Allamandiers

63.6 — **parking, Bordeaux**

8 Créon, St-Émilion & Castillon-la-Bataille

Details:

Distance—77.2 kilometers
Climbing—435 meters
Challenge rank—4.6
Parking: at the Lapébie cycle path near the intersection of D671 and D13.

Bicycle east from Créon 12½ kilometers on the Piste Cyclable Roger Lapébie to the intersection with D122. From that intersection, cycle 12½ kilometers north, crossing the Dordogne Rivière, to St-Émilion. After enjoying lunch with a sip or two of wine in St-Émilion, ride 12 kilometers east and southeast to Castillon-la-Bataille. Then cross back over the Dordogne Rivière and follow it 10 kilometers to St-Jean-de-Blaignac. Stay on the route, looping south and west 16 kilometers to Bellebat, and southwest 12½ kilometers back to Créon.

There are a couple hills: one into St-Émilion and one after St-Jean-de-Blaignac. Neither ascent exceeds 100 meters.

St-Émilion

In an area composed of wine hills and verdant vineyards, this medieval town planted on a limestone prominence benefits from its location at the crossroads of Bordeaux and the Périgord.

Tour du Roy

On average, a million people visit here each year for the hermitage, churches, the archbishop's palace, stately buildings and remains of the fortifications.

They come to appreciate winding streets and shaded squares, enjoy its wine heritage and such gourmet delicacies as macaroons, pies and foie gras.

Église Monolithe de St-Émilion

This UNESCO World Heritage Site is "a remarkable example of an historic vineyard landscape that has survived intact" and "an outstanding example of the intensive cultivation of grapes for wine in a precisely defined region."

Between vineyards and rivers, along wooded hillsides and picturesque roads, St-Émilion stretches over 75 square kilometers around a well-preserved medieval town. This is a set of eight villages organized and united in the Middle Ages around the free town of St-Émilion. It encompasses 7,846 hectares of the wine appellations St-Émilion and St-Émilion Grand Cru, involving 800 wine estates.

The land is divided into five main groups nested within each other. In the center of the appellation is a limestone plateau where in many places the rock is only covered with a thin layer of soil. The slopes are largely planted with vines despite its steepness, and the foot of the slope is clay. Extending to the Dordogne Rivière, the valley consists of sandy loam soil and sandy gravel.

Typical St-Émillion Vineyard

St-Émilion is strongly influenced by agricultural activity, especially wine grapes. The weight of this sector is above the average for the district: it reached 62% against 39% across the area. The construction sector represents a relatively small share of economic activity.

It is the diversity of *terroirs* (loosely defined, lands) that influence the range of the St-Émilion wines. There are three grape varieties: Merlot, which predominates in 60 to 70% of production, cabernet franc and cabernet sauvignon, all for the production of red wines.

The site has evidence of occupation from 35,000 Before the Common Era. A Gallo-Roman villa also existed down the hillside, seemingly for viticulture.

Monastery Ruins

In the eighth century, a native Breton monk named Émilion Valves chose Ascumbas (former name of St-Émilion) as retreat. He left his family and his native Britain to enter the holy orders. Filled with praise and

respect because of his great virtue, Émilion eventually withdrew to Combes in the forest that once covered the present site of St-Émilion.

For seventeen years, Émilion evangelized the population and created a monastic site that was given his name after he died. A community of Benedictine monks managed access to this place of pilgrimage until 1110, when a reform instituted by the Bishop of Bordeaux allowed the installation of a chapter of Augustinian canons.

The town was built during the Middle Ages and was closed by walls in the early thirteenth century.

John Lackland, King of England, established the Jurade in 1199. It used its economic, political and judicial powers, notables and magistrates, to manage the general administration of St-Émilion. In exchange for these privileges, England could enjoy St-Émilion wines. The vineyard area increased with the reputation of the wines. Their quality was subject to review by the Jurade before it was shipped to England from the port of Pierrefitte-la-Dordogne. Through its membership in 1379, the alliance defended Bordeaux against the French troops, and St-Émilion was qualified as the goddaughter of Bordeaux. This alliance encouraged much trade with the capital of the Gironde.

Bacchus, God of the Grape Harvest

The authority of the Jurade lasted until the French Revolution in 1789.

In 1948, growers meeting in the wine trade union revived the Jurade as a brotherhood, which then became the ambassador for the wines of St-Émilion to the world, with the aim to guarantee the authenticity and quality of its wines. It consists of 54 aldermen and is administered by the Board of Jurade, which has twelve members including a clerk, the bagman, the great vinetier and the warden.

On the north edge of the town are remains of an imposing Dominican convent built in the thirteenth century, which included a church, cloister, chapter house and a bell tower. The monks destroyed this convent only a century later, at the beginning of the Hundred Years War, because of its proximity to the town's fortifications. Taken by the enemy, it would have been a strategic point for a siege of the town.

Cobbled Streets

A word of caution: you will want to walk your bicycles due to the very rough cobbled streets and many people wandering (aimlessly?) between the nearly fifty wine shops.

Castillon-la-Bataille

French towns with Castillon in their name suggests a fortified place, but only one has added a term suggesting a battle had marked its history.

The town of Castillon was mentioned about 845: "Castillon is on the river Dordogne," and that it is the seat of Viscount de Castillon created by Charlemagne. Gradually a walled city had developed around a château where you could enter through three portals, one at the edge of the Dordogne Rivière called to this day the Iron Gate.

The Viscount de Castillon depended on the duchy of Aquitaine. In 1152, Duchess Eleanor, after the annulment of her marriage with King Louis VII of France, married Henry Plantagenet who would be crowned King of England two years later. This is the beginning of British rule over Aquitaine, which gave the kings of England the added title as dukes of Aquitaine.

The re-subjugation of Aquitaine by the crown of France was one of the challenges of the Hundred Years War. The last major battle was at Castillon on 17 July 1453. A well-known British military commander, John Talbot, First Earl of Shrewsbury, was killed there. His defeated army fled Castillon, which fell to the French on 20 July. In October, Bordeaux returned to the "obedience of the King of France."

Rue Michel Montaigne

In the following century, the town, then called Castillon en Périgord, faced new problems with the Wars of Religion. The population was predominantly converted to the reformed religion. After a long siege in 1586, the community was defeated and plundered by the Catholic Duke of Mayenne. However, the Protestants resumed their worship the next year.

Despite a relative lull after the Edict of Nantes (1598), disorders did not stop. King Louis XIII had the château and fortifications destroyed in 1624.

The Revolution marked a bloody episode of the banned Girondins (a political faction in France within the Legislative Assembly and the National Convention during The Revolution). Three Girondins were found hiding near Castillon some time before their tragic end at the gates of the city. They committed suicide by gunshot and were found half eaten by wolves.

In 1835 a suspension bridge opened which crossed the Dordogne Rivière. The railway first connected Castillon to Bergerac in 1875, and in 1905 a second bridge was constructed to relieve the old bridge that was in bad repair.

Castillon-la-Bataille

The Second World War saw the arrival of many refugees from eastern France, and the occupation of the city by the German army. Castillon became a frontier town where smugglers were numerous. The Resistance liberated the town.

For the 500th anniversary of the battle of 1453, Castillon changed its name to Castillon-la-Bataille.

Queues and Directions

Segment	Waypoint		Road	Km at start of segment	Km in segment	
①	↑ E		**D803**	0.0	12.4	**Créon**

depart E on Voie Verte Lapebie (D803)

44° 46' 34.33" N	44.77620°	00° 21' 03.57" W	-0.35099°

cross under D20 at 0.4 km — cross D121 at 2.4 km — **98 meters**
cross under D239 at 4.6 km — enter tunnel at 5.2 km
exit tunnel at 5.4 km — cross D140 at 5.8 km
cross D238 at 7.8 km — cross D11e1 at 9.6 km
cross D11 at 11.4 km

Segment	Waypoint		Road	Km	Km in seg	
②	◀⅂ N		**D122**	12.4	5.4	

turn left on D122

44° 47' 19.99" N	44.78889°	00° 12' 57.97" W	-0.21610°

Guillac, cross D128 at 13.8 km — **76 meters**

③	�𝆑▶ E		**D936**	17.8	0.8	**Branne**

turn right on D936

44° 49' 44.92" N	44.82914°	00° 11' 17.03" W	-0.18806°

cross Dordogne Rivière at 18.4 km — **13 meters**

④	◀⅂ N		**D122**	18.6	6.4	

turn left on D122

44° 50' 03.73" N	44.83437°	00° 11' 07.01" W	-0.18528°

cross D670 at 24.2 km — D122e6 on right at 24.6 km — **7 meters**
cross rail line at 24.8 km

⑤	↑ NE			25.0	1.6	**St-Émilion**

straight on Moulin de Palat

44° 53' 07.95" N	44.88554°	00° 09' 24.06" W	-0.15668°

5% ascent — **30 meters**

⑥	�𝆑▶ E		**D243**	26.6	0.2	

turn right on D243

⑦	�𝆑▶ SE		**D243e1**	26.8	2.4	

turn right on D243e1

44° 53' 48.36" N	44.89677°	00° 09' 09.57" W	-0.15266°

75 meters

⑧	�𝆑▶ E		**D243**	29.2	2.2	

turn right on D243

44° 53' 45.98" N	44.89611°	00° 07' 25.53" W	-0.12376°

D243e2 on right at 30.4 km — **83 meters**

⑨	⌐▶ S		**D130**	31.4	5.6	

turn right on D130 — 5% descent

44° 53' 18.09" N	44.88836°	00° 05' 45.94" W	-0.09609°

St-Étienne-de-Lisse, D245 on right at 32.8 km — **66 meters**
St-Magne-de-Castillon at 35.6 km — cross D17e2 at 36.6 km

⑩	⌐▶ SE		**D17**	37.0	1.4	**Castillon-la-Bataille**

turn right on D17

44° 51' 30.89" N	44.85858°	00° 03' 05.02" W	-0.05139°

D123 on right at 37.2 km — cross D936 at 37.6 km — **23 meters**
D936e3 on left at 38.0 km — cross Dordogne Rivière at 38.2 km

⑪	⌐▶ W		**D119**	38.4	9.6	

turn right on D119

44° 50' 58.65" N	44.84963°	00° 02' 34.68" W	-0.04297°

cross D15 at 39.0 km — D119e2 on left at 39.8 km — **9 meters**
Civrac, D126 on left at 42.2 km — D127 on left at 44.6 km

⑫	⌐▶ N		**D670**	48.0	0.2	**St-Jean-de-Blaignac**

turn right on D670

44° 48' 42.26" N	44.81174°	00° 08' 29.65" W	-0.14157°

18 meters

(Waypoints continued on page 26)

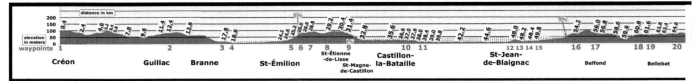

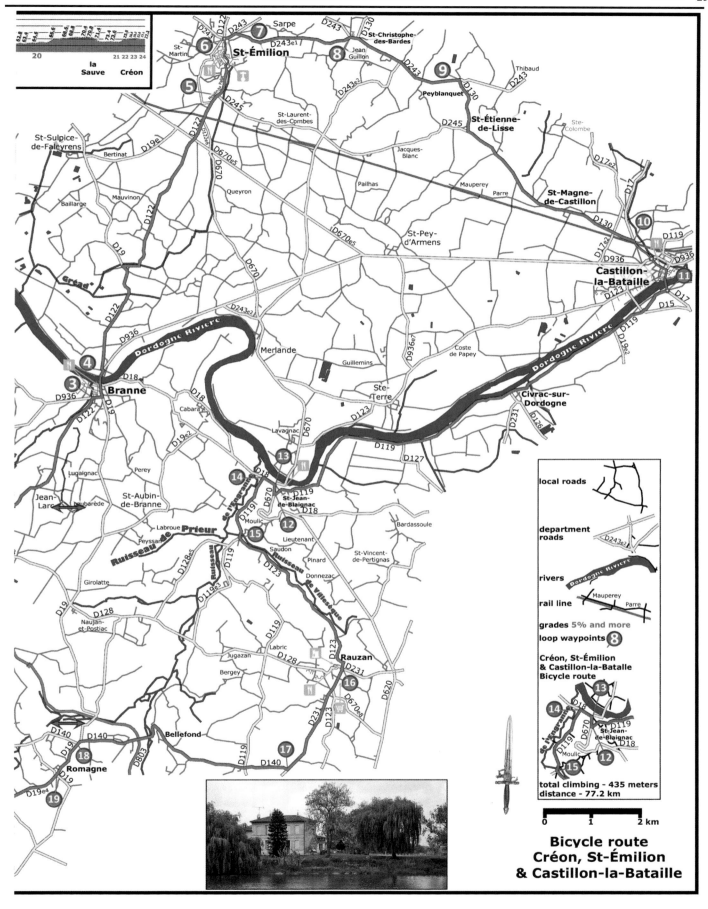

Bicycle route
Créon, St-Émilion
& Castillon-la-Bataille

13 ◄◄ NW   **D18**   48.2   0.4   **St-Jean-de-Blaignac**
turn left on D18

14 ◄ SW   **D119**   48.6   1.2   **St-Jean-de-Blaignac**
turn left on D119

44° 48' 53.58" N	44.81488°	00°	08' 40.89" W	-0.14469°
				9 meters

15 ◄ SE   **D123**   49.8   3.8
turn left on D123

44° 48' 12.64" N	44.80351°	00°	09' 01.91" W	-0.15053°
5% ascent				12 meters

16 ◄/► S   **D231**   53.6   2.4   **Rauzan**
jog left and right on D231, D128 on right

44° 46' 46.04" N	44.77946°	00°	07' 27.64" W	-0.12434°
				68 meters

17 ► W   **D140**   56.0   4.8
turn right on D140

44° 45' 38.66" N	44.76074°	00°	08' 16.33" W	-0.13787°
cross D119 at 56.8 km		**Bellefond** at 58.6 km		79 meters

cross Voie Verte Lapébie (D803) at 59.6 km

18 ◄ SW   **D19**   60.8   0.8
turn left on D19

44° 45' 57.27" N	44.76591°	00°	11' 25.40" W	-0.19039°
				61 meters

19 ↑ SW   **D19e4**   61.6   3.0
straight on D19e4

44° 45' 35.14" N	44.75976°	00°	11' 48.24" W	-0.19673°
D236 on left at 62.8 km		D236 on right at 63.4 km		57 meters

20 ► NW   **D671**   64.6   12.0   **Bellebat**
turn right on D671

44° 44' 25.55" N	44.74043°	00°	13' 02.11" W	-0.21725°
cross D122 at 66.6 km		D11 on right at 68.6 km		69 meters
D11 on left at 68.8 km		D238 on left at 70.4 km		
D238 on right at 70.8 km		D140 on left at 71.4 km		
D239 on right at 73.4 km		**la Sauve**, D239 on left at 73.6 km		

traffic circle, take 2nd exit on D671, D13 at 3rd exit at 75.6 km
Créon at 76.4 km

21 ◉► NE   **D121e5**   76.6   0.1   **Créon**
traffic circle, take 1st exit on D121e5

44° 46' 24.40" N	44.77344°	00°	20' 47.28" W	-0.34647°
				104 meters

22 ◄ S   76.7   0.3   **Créon**
turn left on Rue Guillaume Baudric

23 ◄ SW   77.0   0.1   **Créon**
turn left on Boulevard Victor Hugo

24 ► NW   **D671**   77.1   0.1   **Créon**
turn right on D671

   77.2   parking, **Créon**

St-Émillion Rue de la Liberté

St-Jean-de-Blaignac Mairie

9   Marmande, Duras & la Réole

Details:

Distance—72.0 kilometers

Climbing—595 meters

Challenge rank—5.4

Parking: Boulevard Richard Cœur de Lion in Marmande.

From Boulevard Richard Cœur de Lion and D933e1, bicycle north 23 kilometers to Duras. After Duras, cycle southwest 24½ kilometers to la Réole. Then cross the Garonne Rivière and ride southeast along the Canal du Garonne 12¼ kilometers to waypoint **21**. Follow the route north and east 8½ kilometers across the Garonne Rivière to parking in Marmande

There are no climbs that exceed 100 meters but the route does have five ascents that come close. After climbing the fourth of these, you will understand the total climbing of 595 meters.

Marmande

Richard Cœur de Lion (Richard the Lionheart) established the village as a bastide about 1195. Since it is located on the banks of the Garonne, it was an important place to collect tolls. The Count of Toulouse soon occupied Marmande. Then it was besieged three times and taken during the Albigensian Crusade, a 20-year military campaign initiated by Pope Innocent III to eliminate Catharism in the south of France. Amaury de Montfort captured Marmande in 1219, and then massacred the inhabitants — men, women, the elderly and children. The French crown claimed it under Louis IX. Other important events in its subsequent history include a short occupation by the English in 1447, an unsuccessful siege by Henry IV in 1577 and its resistance of a month to a division of Wellington's army in 1814.

Lévignac-de-Guyenne

On the first Sunday in May (2013), *l'association Le Bouquet aux mille fleurs* (the association Bouquet of a thousand flowers) held its tenth anniversary spring day market.

Flowers and Plants in the Lévignac Market

Large crowds are often found around the many garage sale kiosks. Mushrooms, plants and flowers, along with local produce are for sale.

Lous de Bazats Folk Dancers

The folk group on stilts, Lous de Bazats, danced and walked the streets of the fortified village, while Banda Festiva played tunes with flutes and drums recalling the old Guyenne region.

Duras

Château de Duras

The village is quiet and has one main sight: the Château de Duras. There is also a fourteenth century fortified entry portal and clock tower. Note some attractive houses, plus the Maison des Vins commemorating the highly regarded wines of the region.

The first Duras château was built on a rocky outcrop overlooking the valley in the twelfth century. At the time it was an impregnable fortress.

Both the English and French fought to occupy it during the Hundred Years War. During the Wars of Religion, it was a bastion of Jeanne d'Albret, the sixteenth century queen regent of Navarre and mother of Henry IV, the first Bourbon king.

In the seventeenth century, it was the residence of the Dukes of Duras. It was at that time that the Château de Duras turned into a pleasure palace to which they added the French gardens.

Château Entrance

In 1969, the community of Duras bought it.

The main building is a quadrangle flanked by four round towers at the corners. In the seventeenth century two buildings with superimposed galleries were built on existing foundations. These formed the north and south sides of the courtyard.

The former backyard from the fourteenth century, by the corner tower, has a chapel and is adjacent to a small château located south of the forecourt of the main building.

Also important are the cooler, kitchen, carpentry details, the terraces and retaining walls.

Côtes de Duras is an Appellation d'Origine Contrôlée (AOC) for local red and white wines. The area also produces a small amount of rosé and medium-sweet white wines.

There are at least six restaurants along with a popular bar serving sandwiches in the village.

la Réole

The community was chartered as a monastery, according to a questionable founding document, in 977. This document shows how the monks tried to establish their privileges on the secular society of nobles and the burghers of Réole.

Much history of the Middle Ages comes down to this double conflict between monks on the one hand, and nobility and bourgeoisie on the other. At each escalation of the conflict, the city became a battlefield, sometimes inside, usually at the foot of the walls. Typically, the conflict ended in favor of the bourgeoisie, which mastered the art of selling their loyalty to the highest bidder.

The pivotal position of Réole in the long struggle between the rulers of France and England was like a seesaw and sometimes risky, but always favorable to the small bourgeois society that dominated the city.

In 1004, Abbo, renowned theologian and abbot of Fleury-sur-Loire came to Réole. His mission was to restore order in the priory where the accumulation of wealth had led to a relaxation of discipline. He was killed during a violent quarrel, as it was reported, between the Benedictines.

Richard the Lionheart was the Duke of Aquitaine before becoming the King of England. As such, he visited Réole more than once.

In 1224, the Réolais receive from King Louis VIII permission to build a fortress in the southwest corner of the city. Thus, the city built the Castle Quat'Sos (four sisters, because of the identical appearance of its four corner towers) on the promontory overlooking the confluence of the Garonne and its tiny tributary the Charros. The fortress, the priory and the riches of the city became one of the stakes of the struggle that continued between the kings of France and England until the final victory by the French at Castillon-la-Bataille in 1453.

la Réole Bridge and Garonne Rivière

Since Paleolithic times, the Garonne valley downstream from Toulouse played an important role: the passageway between the Atlantic plains and the shores of the Mediterranean. As elsewhere in Europe, the path of men often brought destruction and exacerbated the risk of prosperity and development.

The founders of Réole wanted to reconcile all the advantages of the location along the Garonne while reducing risk by choosing an easily defensible site. For much of its length, the valley is bordered on its right side by a steep hillside. And at Réole, the river is at the foot of the hill.

For centuries, the river life was inseparable from that of the inhabitants. Multiple floods have left indelible marks on the walls and in the collective memory. The annual alternating high water during winter and low water in summer are part of the history. Major floods, three or four times a century, are experienced that challenge companies without changing their aspirations. Only houses on the waterfront and those located in a nearby suburb on the other banks have flooded.

A few meters back, the strength of the escarpment provides protection from flooding. This natural balcony is basically beyond the reach of the river and defended Réole to the south. To the west and in the east of the original site, two valleys also provide natural protection.

Browse the market on Saturday morning, as old as the city itself, where regular customers and vendors come from a ten miles radius. At various times, this area grew or shrank, but it never disappeared.

At the end of feudal wars, Réolais experienced a long period of calm except when it was seriously affected by the Wars of Religion (i.e. the ruin of the city by the Huguenots in 1577) and, to a lesser extent, by troop movements in 1649 and 1653.

The Château de Quat'Sos retains its name, but only three of its towers remain, more or less shortened, and its walls were demolished over half of their perimeter. By dismantling the fortresses of provincial nobility, Richelieu ensured their submission to the royal power. This is what he did to Réole in 1629, not without expelling those who opposed it.

The Garonne Rivière continues to play its role as a privileged communication channel, from antiquity to the nineteenth century. The main goods that were carried downstream included wheat and wine from Cahors. Commerce upstream was salt.

A flotilla of small boats allowed Réole to expand its sphere of influence on the opposite bank before the construction of a bridge.

Réole at the middle of the eighteenth century resembled the transformation of Paris under Baron Haussmann. The priory was being rebuilt, the walls were partially demolished and their stones reused here and there. In addition, a large number of old houses in the center were renovated or rebuilt. Solid stone buildings of two to four levels were built. The opulent houses of the sixteenth century (the Black Prince hotel) and the seventeenth century (hotel Briet) dominated a landscape still half rural. The mansions of the eighteenth century multiplied.

The turmoil of The Revolution did not spare Réole. After drawn-out discussions on departmental boundaries (there was even talk of defining a department Réole-Bazas) during The Revolution, Réole became a sub-prefecture in 1800.

In 1834, the first wooden bridge that connects the two banks of the Garonne was commissioned, and ended a very old activity, the smugglers and their boats. It was exactly one hundred years later, in 1934, that a suspension bridge was built according to the most advanced techniques for the time. Today, this bridge is completely saturated with traffic (ride with care). A new bridge now crosses the river one kilometer upstream for regional traffic.

In the mid-nineteenth century, two major projects were conducted simultaneously: the Canal de Garonne and the railway from Bordeaux to Tonneins. If the route of the canal does not affect Réole directly, the commissioning dealt a heavy blow to the river port traffic. It continued to decline until early in the twentieth century, before disappearing completely.

Canal de Garonne and Voie Verte

The construction of the railway was spectacular for the city. Despite the obstacles of terrain and density of housing, the route passes under the front of the priory into a first tunnel, then emerges to cross the valley on a viaduct with two arches and enters a second tunnel that is three hundred meters long. Much more than the canal, the rail line caused the decline and death of the river traffic on the Garonne. Inaugurated in 1855, the line was quickly connected to the national grid and has continued with upgrades to the current period, on the same route. The canal, which has never had traffic comparable to the north of France river systems, is now a tourist attraction helping the economy.

elevation in meters
waypoints

5%
4.2
5% to 7%
distance in km
16.0
22.8
23.2
23.1
24.0
24.1
27.8
32.4
34.8
37.0
46.8
47.4
47.8
48.2
49.6
49.d
51.2

1 2   3   5 6 7 8 9   10   11   12   13   15 16 17 18 19 20

Beaupuy
Marmande
5% to 6%
5%
Lévignac-
sur-Guyenne
5% to 7%
Duras
5%
St-Hilaire-
de-la-Noaille
la
Réole

local roads
department roads
rail line
rivers
grades 5% and more
loop waypoints 8

Marmande, Duras
& la Réole
Bicycle route

Duras

total climbing - 595 meters
distance - 72.0 km

© WALTER JUDSON MOORE

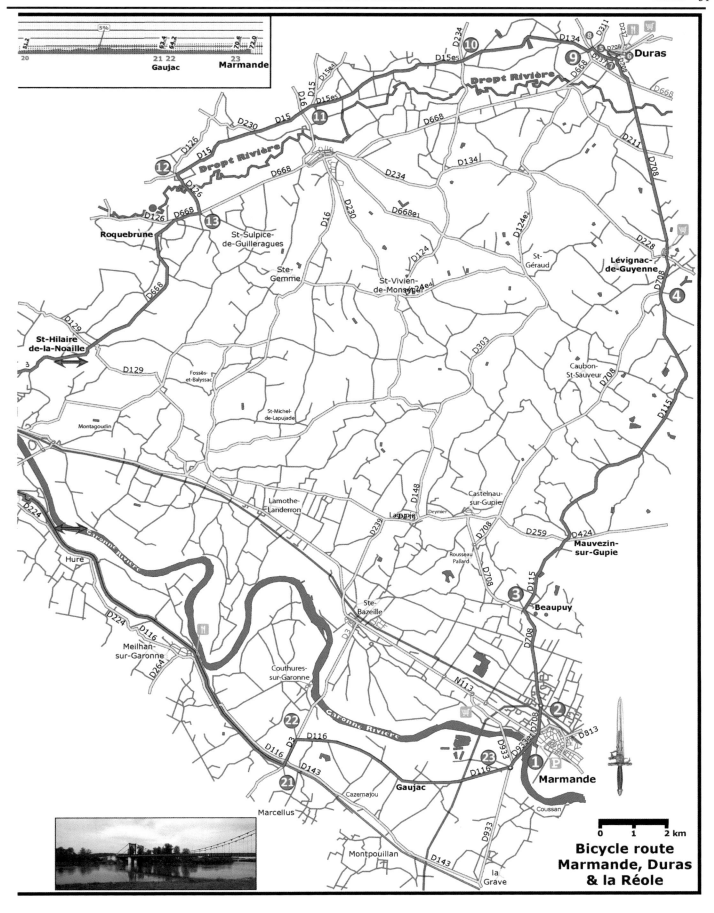

Gaujac   Marmande

Dropt Rivière

Dropt Rivière

Duras

Roquebrune

St-Sulpice-
de-Guilleragues

St-Hilaire
de-la-Noaille

Ste-
Gemme

St-Vivien-
de-Monségur

St-Géraud

Lévignac-
de-Guyenne

Caubon-
St-Sauveur

Fossès-
et-Balyssac

St-Michel-
de-Lapujade

Montagoudin

Lamothe-
Landerron

Castelnau-
sur-Gupie

Deymier

Lagupie

Mauvezin-
sur-Gupie

Rousseau
Pallard

Hure

Garonne Rivière

Beaupuy

Ste-
Bazeille

Meilhan-
sur-Garonne

Couthures-
sur-Garonne

Garonne Rivière

Marmande

Gaujac

Cazernajou

Coussan

Marcellus

Montpouillan

la
Grave

0   1   2 km

**Bicycle route
Marmande, Duras
& la Réole**

Queues and Directions

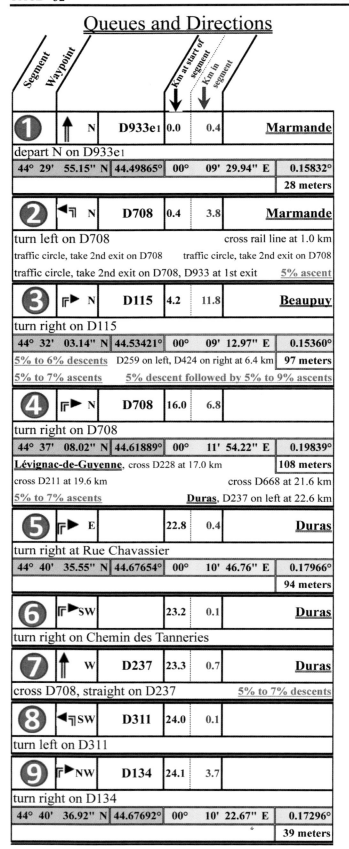

(Diagram labels: Segment · Waypoint · Km at start of segment · Km in segment)

① ↑ N D933e1 0.0 0.4 Marmande
depart N on D933e1
44° 29' 55.15" N | 44.49865° | 00° 09' 29.94" E | 0.15832°
28 meters

② ◀ N D708 0.4 3.8 Marmande
turn left on D708 — cross rail line at 1.0 km
traffic circle, take 2nd exit on D708 — traffic circle, take 2nd exit on D708
traffic circle, take 2nd exit on D708, D933 at 1st exit — 5% ascent

③ ▶ N D115 4.2 11.8 Beaupuy
turn right on D115
44° 32' 03.14" N | 44.53421° | 00° 09' 12.97" E | 0.15360°
5% to 6% descents — D259 on left, D424 on right at 6.4 km — 97 meters
5% to 7% ascents — 5% descent followed by 5% to 9% ascents

④ ▶ N D708 16.0 6.8
turn right on D708
44° 37' 08.02" N | 44.61889° | 00° 11' 54.22" E | 0.19839°
Lévignac-de-Guyenne, cross D228 at 17.0 km — 108 meters
cross D211 at 19.6 km — cross D668 at 21.6 km
5% to 7% ascents — Duras, D237 on left at 22.6 km

⑤ ▶ E   22.8 0.4 Duras
turn right at Rue Chavassier
44° 40' 35.55" N | 44.67654° | 00° 10' 46.76" E | 0.17966°
94 meters

⑥ ▶ SW   23.2 0.1 Duras
turn right on Chemin des Tanneries

⑦ ↑ W D237 23.3 0.7 Duras
cross D708, straight on D237 — 5% to 7% descents

⑧ ◀ SW D311 24.0 0.1
turn left on D311

⑨ ▶ NW D134 24.1 3.7
turn right on D134
44° 40' 36.92" N | 44.67692° | 00° 10' 22.67" E | 0.17296°
39 meters

⑩ ↑ SW D15e5 27.8 4.6
straight on D15e5
44° 40' 27.98" N | 44.67444° | 00° 07' 43.62" E | 0.12878°
30 meters

⑪ ↑ SW D15 32.4 2.4
straight on D15
44° 39' 45.82" N | 44.66273° | 00° 04' 33.43" E | 0.07595°
cross D16 at 32.8 km — D230 on right at 34.2 km — 33 meters

⑫ ◀ S D126 34.8 3.2
turn left on D126
44° 38' 42.62" N | 44.64517° | 00° 01' 45.78" E | 0.02938°
cross Dropt Rivière at 35.2 km — 24 meters

⑬ ▶ W D668 38.0 8.8
turn right on D668
44° 38' 08.70" N | 44.63575° | 00° 02' 09.39" E | 0.03594°
D126 on right at 38.6 km — 23 meters
St-Hilaire-de-la-Noaille, cross D129 at 43.6 km

⑭ ◀● S D670 46.8 0.6 la Réole
traffic circle, take 3rd exit on D670, D670 also at 1st exit
44° 35' 30.57" N | 44.59183° | 00° 01' 57.15" W | -0.03254°
74 meters

⑮ ▶ S D668 47.4 0.4 la Réole
turn right on D668

⑯ ↑ W   47.8 0.4 la Réole
cross D9 & D1113, straight on Rue Armand Caduc
5% descent

⑰ ◀ S   48.2 0.4 la Réole
left around Église St-Pierre toward D9e1

⑱ ◀ E D9e1 48.6 0.8 la Réole
turn left on D9e1

⑲ ▶ S D9e6 49.4 1.8
turn right on D9e6, cross Garonne Rivière
44° 34' 46.38" N | 44.57955° | 00° 02' 02.42" W | -0.03401°
cross D9 at 50.8 km — cross Canal de Garonne at 51.2 km — 18 meters

20	◀⌐ SE		51.2	12.2	
turn left on Voie Verte de Canal du Garonne					
44° 33' 49.10" N	44.56364°	00°	01' 47.58" W	-0.02988°	
cross Canal du Garonne at 54.6 km				21 meters	
cross Canal du Garonne at 57.8 km		cross Canal du Garonne at 57.8 km			
cross Canal du Garonne at 59.0 km		cross D116 at 61.0 km			
21	◀⌐ NE	D3	63.4	0.8	
turn left on D3					
44° 29' 34.88" N	44.49302°	00°	04' 12.12" E	0.07003°	
				26 meters	
22	⌐▶ NE	D116	64.2	6.4	
turn right on D116					
44° 29' 57.66" N	44.49935°	00°	04' 28.57" E	0.07460°	
Gaujac at 67.4 km		cross under rail line at 69.2 km		18 meters	
23	⟳▶ N	D933e1	70.6	1.4	
traffic circle, take 2nd exit on D933e1, D933 at 1st exit					
44° 29' 33.91" N	44.49275°	00°	08' 59.66" E	0.14991°	
cross Garonne Rivière at 71.4 km				23 meters	
			72.0	parking, Marmande	

Marmande Waterfront

Duras View

Lévignac-de-Guyenne Church During Sunday Market

Dropt Rivière Near Roquebrune

10 Seyches & Eymet

Details:

Distance—57.9 kilometers

Climbing—455 meters

Challenge rank—3.8

Parking: Marché Fermier parking lot at the intersection of D933 & D228 in Seyches.

Bicycle northwest and north through Allemans-du-Dropt. After Allemans continue north to Moustier and northeast to Eymet. Next cycle southeast to Lauzun, and south and southwest through St-Barthélemy-d'Agenais to Agmé. Follow the route northwest through Puymiclan to Seyches.

Seyches East Portal

There are no climbs exceeding 100 meters on this route, and only three 5% to 6% grades.

Dropt Rivière

The Dropt Rivière became significant starting in the thirteenth century and through the fifteenth century as the border between territories of the Counts of Toulouse and dukes of Aquitaine, and thus kings of England. Both sides adopted a strategy of establishing the border by creating new towns along the river.

The Dropt has 66 dams for 75 mills. Mills still in operation are rare. The rest have been stripped of their machines. Most have been converted to primary or secondary residences.

Downstream of Eymet, the dams include locks, which are remnants of the days when the Dropt was navigable. The Dropt, as a tributary of the Garonne,

abandoned barge navigation during the expansion of railways.

The river is 64 kilometers long with 34 kilometers still navigable.

Dropt Rivière Near Allemans-du-Dropt

Allemans-du-Dropt

The village is on the left bank of Dropt Rivière, which was the border that separated the Celts of Agen in the late third century Before the Common Era, and the Pétrocoriens of the Dordogne valley. The village name came from a tribe of Germanic Alemanni who invaded the region in the early sixth century of the Common Era.   It is difficult to specify the establishment date of the village, but it probably took place before the year 1000. The village at the time included the château, the church and its adjoining cemetery, a single street lined with houses and the inner hall, which belonged to the lords.

Allemans Mill

At the end of the fifteenth century, the mill existed on the Dropt.   More recently, Allemans was affected by the wars of the nineteenth and twentieth centuries. During World War II, many Alsatian families found refuge in the area.

 The mill vaults of the tailrace suggest that construction dates back to the thirteenth and fourteenth centuries. It was rebuilt and elevated during the nineteenth and twentieth centuries to meet demand. It ceased service in 1967.

Eymet

Located in a meander of the Dropt Rivière, the medieval village marks the southern entrance of the old Périgord Region. The political entity came into being on 28 June 1270 as a bastide. Alphonse de Poitiers, Count of Toulouse and brother of St. Louis, was responsible. Eymet changed hands several times during the Hundred Years Wars. This was finally settled by the Battle of Castillon and the re-conquest of the Aquitaine by the French King Charles VII in 1453.

Winner of Aquitaine's *Plan Bastide* competition, Eymet has preserved and developed a heritage of medieval times with attractive proportions surrounded by arcaded houses. Streets intersect at right angles with many half-timbered houses and Gothic buildings.

Old Wharf Vestiges

The remains of the navigation wharf reminds visitors that Eymet was a port where small barges from Bordeaux were loaded with wood, wine and grains. The fourteenth century mill is also evidence of a significant commercial activity in recent centuries. Cycle through the heart of the village to discover the arcades and paths of the old town.

Eymet also has a private fortified château near the Dropt and north of the mill.

Back to Alphonse de Poitiers: in 1271, he died without an heir. Toulouse and Agen were returned to the crown of France, as per the 1229 Treaty of Meaux. Eymet became French, but the Treaty of Amiens transferred Agen to England eight years later. The region spent more time in the hands of the dreaded English bandit lord, Gilbert de Pellegrue.

The chronicler Froissart wrote about a battle of 1 September 1377, when a commander du Guesclin of the Duke of Anjou's troops, had just taken back from the English many defensives positions, towns and châteaux in Aquitaine. Du Guesclin put a strongly fortified Bergerac under siege, although the king's steward Thomas Felton defended it. To demolish the Bergerac walls, du Guesclin acquired an engine of war called *la truye*, a sort of huge ram that was pushed by more than 100 men.

Warned in advance, Felton set up an ambush for the convoy at the approaches to Eymet. Hearing about the ambush, du Guesclin ordered his lieutenant to attack the enemy troops. A large number of English were drowned in the Dropt Rivière, just South of Eymet, at a place called The Englishmen's Hole.

Place des Arcades

Felton was captured, but was soon freed after payment of a ransom. The convoy tried to leave but the ram was blocked at Eymet's southern gate, which was too narrow and had to be partially demolished. This gate from then on was called Gate of the Engine and the street that leads to it is still called *Rue de l'Engin*.

History does record the exact date of the end of the British presence in Eymet, but does remember the date June 1451 marking the submission of Gilbert Pellegrue to King of France Charles VII, two years before the Battle of Castillon, which marked the official end of the Hundred Years War and 300 years of British presence in Aquitaine.

Lauzun

Lauzun was the location of a Gallo-Roman fortress. A fortified château was probably constructed here in the sixth century. The Lords of Gontaut became lords of Lauzun in the twelfth century. The Caumont de la Force de Lauzun lords were the rulers at the end of the Middle Ages. The château became the property of Charles IX and Catherine de Medici in 1565.

(Continued on page 38)

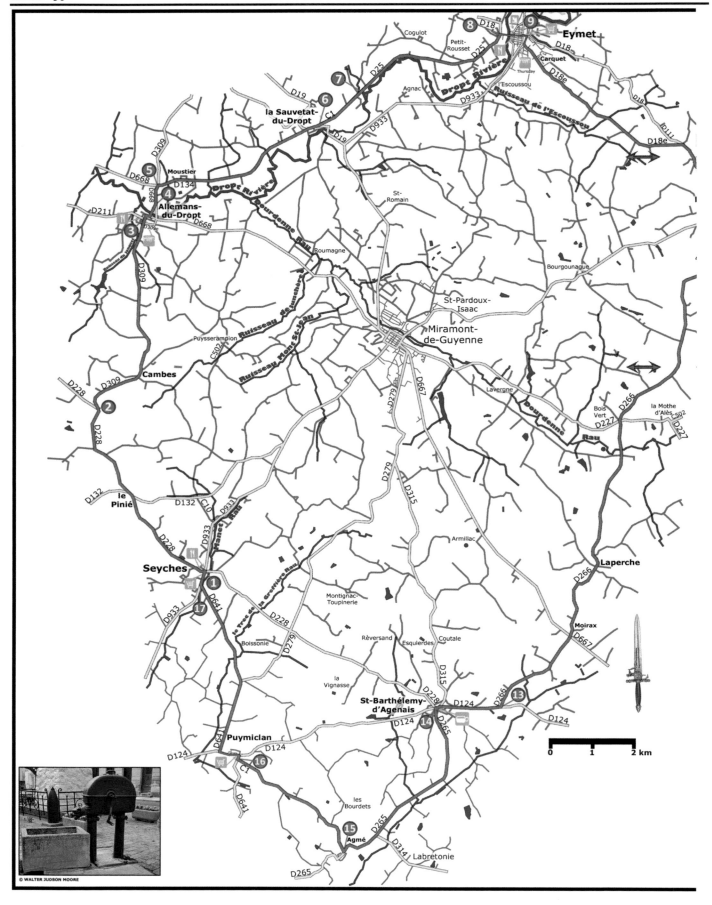

© WALTER JUDSON MOORE

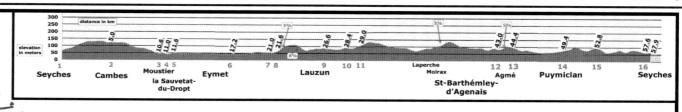

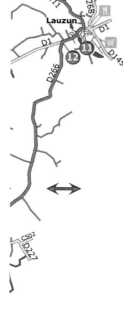

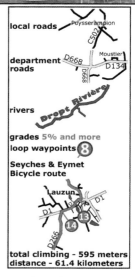

local roads
department roads
rivers
grades 5% and more
loop waypoints
Seyches & Eymet
Bicycle route

total climbing - 595 meters
distance - 61.4 kilometers

**Bicycle route
Seyches & Eymet**

At the entrance of the village on the route coming from Eymet on the right inside of a turn, it is possible to observe trees on a mound of earth about ten meters high (with better eyes than mine). Long, the locals thought it was a tumulus, a mound of cone-shaped earth that ancestors placed above graves. Indeed, it seems that this hill is from the Middle Ages. If true, it would be a mound on which stood feudal wooden fortifications.

In the thirteenth century there was a dungeon and a 20-meter by 10-meter building that was the old chapel. A fortified château is mentioned for the first time in 1259. In 1305, Edward I, King of England, authorized Peter I of Gontaut to elevate and strengthen the Château de Lauzun. At the end of the Middle Ages, the manor belonged to Caumont. The empty space between the bay and the dungeon is filled by an extension of the fifteenth century, on the north side of the dungeon. This expansion included a turret that has been preserved and can be seen east across the lake at the west of the village.

Château de Lauzun

The Château de Lauzun suffered during The Revolution. In August 1811, Joseph N. Becquey-Beaupré bought château. He continued the destruction by the Duke at the end of The Revolution. The stones were sold and used for other buildings. Becquey-Beaupré demolished all defensive elements, but kept the thirteenth century terraces along with the walls on the south and east. On the death of Mr. Becquey-Beaupré, his widow and three children continued to live in the castle for a few years. She then sold it to the Lauzun mayor on 23 October 1837.

The château remained in the Charrié family between 1837 and 1921. Henry inherited the property around the château, which included many farms. The Renaissance wing has been well preserved, with its door and its two chimneys, which have been regularly maintained.

After the death of their father, the château and the properties went to his two children, Jean and Henriette Charrié. They realized that they could not maintain the château and properties, and keep them in decent shape. As a result, they decided to sell the property in 1920. At that time, in addition to the château and its park, the property consisted of five farms of about 30 hectares each. These farms produced grain, plus a few hectares of vines and plums. The first sale was canceled, as the buyer was penniless. A second sale took place in September 1921.

The Église St-Etienne is in the block northwest of the château. All that remains of the original Romanesque church is the portal with seven arches and a late thirteenth century pointed arch. The portal was modified in the sixteenth century to include a statue of the crowned Virgin. The church was rebuilt between 1866 and 1871 with elevation of the vault. The front of the altar represents the Adoration of the Magi. Beside the twisted columns on each side, one sees the angel Gabriel saluting the Virgin. The panels of the pulpit are from 1623. On the altar of the Virgin is a black Virgin dating from the thirteenth century, *Nostro Damo de la Molo* (Our Lady of the wheel) that Lord de Lauzun supposedly found in a haystack, and which was the object of pilgrimage on the road to Compostela. To the left of the altar is a Madonna and Child dating from the thirteenth century. A seventeenth century crystal and silver Reliquary of the True Cross is also in the church.

Queues and Directions

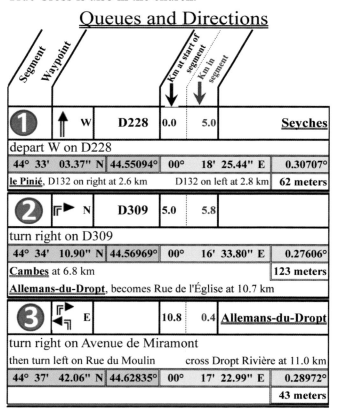

Segment	Waypoint			Km at start of segment	Km in segment	
①	⬆	W	D228	0.0	5.0	**Seyches**
depart W on D228						
44° 33' 03.37" N	44.55094°	00°	18'	25.44" E		0.30707°
le Pinié, D132 on right at 2.6 km			D132 on left at 2.8 km			62 meters
②	⬏	N	D309	5.0	5.8	
turn right on D309						
44° 34' 10.90" N	44.56969°	00°	16'	33.80" E		0.27606°
Cambes at 6.8 km						123 meters
Allemans-du-Drop, becomes Rue de l'Église at 10.7 km						
③	⬏⬐	E		10.8	0.4	**Allemans-du-Drop**
turn right on Avenue de Miramont						
then turn left on Rue du Moulin			cross Dropt Rivière at 11.0 km			
44° 37' 42.06" N	44.62835°	00°	17'	22.99" E		0.28972°
						43 meters

④ ◄⌐ N | D668 | 11.2 | 0.4

turn left on D668

---

⑤ ⌐► E | D134 | 11.6 | 4.2

turn right on D134

44° 38' 04.89" N	44.63469°	00°	17' 34.80" E	0.29300°
Moustier at 12.2 km				48 meters
D19 on left at 15.6 km				

---

⑥ ↑ NE | C1 | 15.8 | 1.4 | la Sauvetat-du-Dropt

straight on C1

44° 38' 51.77" N	44.64771°	00°	20' 26.49" E	0.34069°
D19 on right at 16.0 km				45 meters

---

⑦ ↑ NE | D25 | 17.2 | 3.8

straight on D25

44° 39' 17.40" N	44.65483°	00°	21' 07.20" E	0.35200°
				44 meters

---

⑧ ⌐► E | D18 | 21.0 | 0.6 | Eymet

turn right on D18, cross Dropt Rivière

44° 40' 01.50" N	44.66708°	00°	23' 33.63" E	0.39268°
				52 meters

---

⑨ ◄⌐ / ⌐► S | D18e | 21.6 | 5.0 | Eymet

jog left and right across D933, right on D18e

44° 40' 00.17" N	44.66671°	00°	24' 00.98" E	0.40027°
5% ascent, then 6% descents				57 meters

---

⑩ ⌐► SE | D111 | 26.6 | 1.8

turn right on D111

44° 38' 35.99" N	44.64333°	00°	26' 43.62" E	0.44545°
				81 meters

---

⑪ ⌐► W | D1 | 28.4 | 0.6 | Lauzun

turn right on D1

44° 37' 49.03" N	44.63029°	00°	27' 34.89" E	0.45969°
				87 meters

---

⑫ ◄⌐ S | D266 | 29.0 | 14.0

turn left on D266

44° 37' 38.40" N	44.62733°	00°	27' 11.97" E	0.45333°
cross D277 34.8 km			5% ascent	79 meters
Laperche at 38.6 km			Moirax at 40.4 km	
cross D667 at 40.6				

---

⑬ ⌐► W | D124 | 43.0 | 1.6

turn right on D124

44° 31' 20.90" N	44.52247°	00°	23' 33.32" E	0.39259°
D315 on right at 44.4 km				78 meters

---

⑭ ◄⌐ S | D265 | 44.6 | 4.8 | St-Barthélemy-d'Agenais

turn left on D265, D228 on right

44° 31' 20.02" N	44.52223°	00°	22' 26.66" E	0.37407°
D314 on left at 48.4 km				91 meters

---

⑮ ⌐► N | | 49.4 | 3.4 | Agmé

turn right toward Puymiclan

44° 29' 29.83" N	44.49162°	00°	20' 51.80" E	0.34772°
				73 meters

---

⑯ ⌐► N | D641 | 52.8 | 4.8 | Puymiclan

turn right on D641

44° 30' 40.09" N	44.51114°	00°	19' 00.92" E	0.31692°
D124 straight ahead at 53.4 km		D279 on right at 55.2 km		89 meters

---

⑰ ⌐► N | D933 | 57.6 | 0.3

turn right on D933

44° 32' 54.95" N	44.54860°	00°	18' 21.99" E	0.30611°
				59 meters

			57.9	parking, Seyches

Eymet Restaurant and Shops

11 Miramont-de-Guyenne, Castillonnès & Monbahus

Details:

Distance—60.8 kilometers

Climbing—505 meters

Challenge rank—4.3

Parking: public parking lot at the intersection of D120 and D124 in Tombebœuf.

Bicycle northwest 13½ kilometers to Miramont-de-Guyenne. After Miramont, cycle northeast 21½ kilometers through Lauzun to Castillonnès. Next, ride south then southwest 25½ kilometers through Monbahus back to Tombebœuf.

There are no climbs exceeding 100 meters on this route, and only three 5% to 6% grades.

Miramont-de-Guyenne

The village was founded between 1278 and 1286, was known as Miramont de Lauzun and was a bastide of the Duke of Lauzun.

Like many communities in the area, it forms an almost perfect rectangle with its four main streets intersecting around the central square. The arcades around the square housed stores for merchants in the Middle Ages. Now, multi centuries later, the arcades serve the same purpose.

Place de l'Hôtel de Ville

These bastides were built on the plan of a Roman camp with an arcaded square occupying the center. In the center there was the hall with the first floor a common house. The streets intersected at right angles and the wall, topped with square towers, was protected by a moat.

Miramont was under the administration of Alphonse de Poitiers (1220 — 1271), brother of St-Louis, and experienced one of the more prosperous periods in its history. The English returned in 1259. Miramont was already at that time, a peaceful and industrial town. During the Hundred Years War, the city was repeatedly destroyed and its inhabitants scattered in the neighboring countryside. In 1453, when the French had regained the Guyenne, Miramont rose gradually from its ruins and in 1494 Charles VIII restored its former fortified status and authorized the election of two consuls responsible for raising and distributing taxes.

Throughout religious wars and revolution Miramont suffered. It was not until the Restoration that it reclaimed its industrial past including the manufacture of fine sheepskin slippers. After World War II, changing techniques and competition required modernization of the shoe making equipment and specialized workers. Soon "shoes Miramont" acquired a national reputation for elegance and quality that made the city a recognized metropolis of the shoe.

Lauzun

The site of the village was the location of an oppidum in the Gallo-Roman period. This strength allowed the occupants to defend the land and outbuildings. At the end of the sixth century, a château was built. Serfs, artisans and traders settled around it.

From the twelfth century, the lords of Caumont de Lauzun ruled Lauzun and the surrounding land. A hundred years later, the château became a fortress with a dungeon, ramparts, moats and drawbridges, and was defended by towers.

Église St-Etienne

2

Château de Lauzun

Over time, improvements and modifications were made, and the château was changed during the Renaissance into a comfortable mansion. At the end of the Middle Ages, the Lords of Lauzun had some eighteen churches and chapels, but unfortunately these religious buildings were abandoned or destroyed during the Wars of Religion and then throughout The Revolution.

Part of Lauzun's history includes Armand Louis de Gontaut-Biron, Duc de Lauzun who was born in Paris on 13 April 1747. As General Biron, he participated in the War of Independence in the United States with his Hussars Lauzun under the command of Rochambeau. He led his troops and participated with gallantry at the siege of Yorktown in October 1781, which was one of the war's decisive victories. After returning to France, he was caught up in the rumors concerning the lovers of Marie-Antoinette. Also, he joined The Revolution as a lieutenant general in 1792. Biron commanded the armies of the West against the Vendee in 1793. Accused of treason, he and his head parted company at the blade of the guillotine on 31 December 1793 in Paris' Place de la Revolution.

Castillonnès

The village has a typical bastide layout with a central cloistered square and a church at one corner. The name Castillonnès comes from the French, *castillo neu* (new castle) and refers to its origins on the site of a much older ruined château that was built on a high rocky outcrop. The town plan was developed by Alphonse de Poitiers to follow the natural contours of the hill.

Building began in 1259 just before the start of the Hundred Years War.

Maison de Poitiers

As well as the traditional market place in the arcades of the town square, Castillonnès also has a covered hall and clock tower.

Monbahus

The early history of the village is sketchy. That said, Monbahus was a fortified community founded in the eleventh or twelfth century, built on a hill with farms to the south. A place called the Fort with a motte and bailey (that is, a fortification with a wooden or stone keep situated on a raised earthwork called a motte, accompanied by an enclosed courtyard, or bailey), surrounded by a protective ditch and palisade was confirmed to some by an old oral history.

Monahus Mairie and Church

(Continued on page 44)

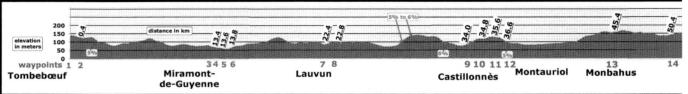

© WALTER JUDSON MOORE

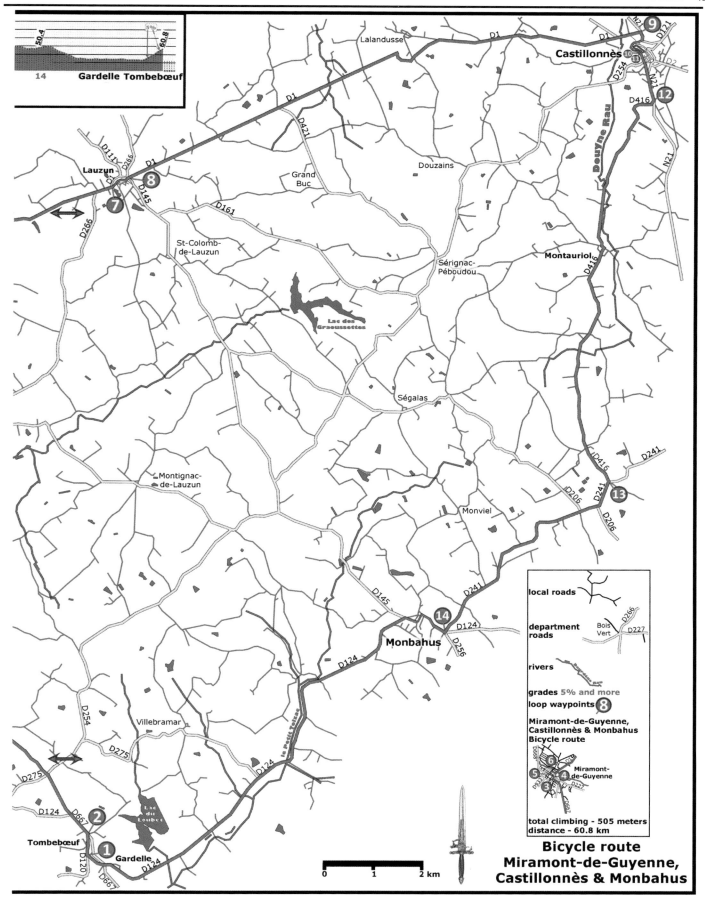

Gardelle Tombebœuf

Lalandusse

D1

Castillonnès

Douzains

Grand
Buc

Montauriol

Sérignac-
Péboudou

Lauzun

St-Colomb-
de-Lauzun

Lac des
Graoussettes

Deuyne Rau

Ségalas

Montignac-
de-Lauzun

Monviel

Monbahus

Villebramar

Lac du
Loubet

Tombebœuf

Gardelle

local roads

department
roads

rivers

grades 5% and more

loop waypoints 8

Miramont-de-Guyenne,
Castillonnès & Monbahus
Bicycle route

Bois
Vert

Miramont-
de-Guyenne

total climbing - 505 meters
distance - 60.8 km

0   1   2 km

**Bicycle route
Miramont-de-Guyenne,
Castillonnès & Monbahus**

Above Monbahus four windmills were located on the ridge in the early seventeenth century and eighteenth century, and listed on the Napoleonic cadastral map of the time. Three mills were demolished between 1876 and 1891. The mill Galinat was given by a notary to the parish in 1898, which decided to transform it into a chapel known as Notre-Dame de la Butte du Moulin and crown it with a monumental statue of the Virgin.

Notre-Dame de la Butte du Moulin

In the early nineteenth century the village consisted of the church, the hall and a group of about twenty houses. It had a terrace on the north side of the hill. Several houses facing the hall still had covered ground floor porches, perhaps for livestock.

Queues and Directions

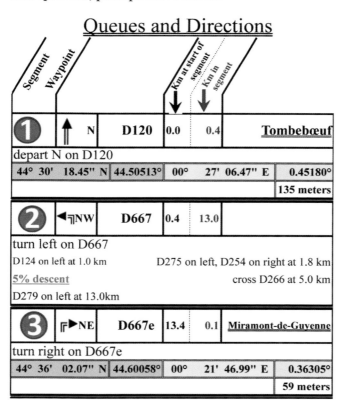

Segment	Waypoint	Road	Km at start of segment	Km in segment	Town
1	↑ N	D120	0.0	0.4	**Tombebœuf**
depart N on D120					
44° 30' 18.45" N	44.50513°	00°	27' 06.47" E		0.45180°
					135 meters
2	◀ NW	D667	0.4	13.0	
turn left on D667					
D124 on left at 1.0 km			D275 on left, D254 on right at 1.8 km		
5% descent			cross D266 at 5.0 km		
D279 on left at 13.0km					
3	▶ NE	D667e	13.4	0.1	**Miramont-de-Guyenne**
turn right on D667e					
44° 36' 02.07" N	44.60058°	00°	21' 46.99" E		0.36305°
					59 meters

Segment	Waypoint	Road	Km at start of segment	Km in segment	Town
4	◀ NW		13.5	0.1	**Miramont-de-Guyenne**
turn left on Rue Pasteur, D277 on right					
5	▶ NE		13.6	0.1	**Miramont-de-Guyenne**
turn right on Rue Bernard Palissy					
6	▶ SE	D1	13.7	8.7	**Miramont-de-Guyenne**
turn right on D1 (Blvd Gambetta)					
St-Pardoux-Isaac at 14.8 km			**Bourgougnague** at 18.8 km		
7	▶ E		22.4	0.4	**Lauzun**
turn right on Rue du 19 Mars					
44° 37' 41.75" N	44.62826°	00°	27' 25.56" E		0.45710°
becomes Rue Pissebaque at 22.6 km					**87 meters**
8	◀ NE	D1	22.8	11.2	**Lauzun**
turn left on Rue Marcel Hervé, jog right on D1					
D421 on right at 26.2 km			5% to 6% ascent		
6% descent			D288 on left at 33.6 km		
9	▶ S	N21	34.0	0.8	
turn right on N21					
44° 39' 26.97" N	44.65749°	00°	35' 23.44" E		0.58984°
D121 on left at 34.2 km					**79 meters**
10	◀ E		34.8	0.8	**Castillonnès**
turn left on Promenade de la Mouthe through **Castillonnès**					
44° 39' 10.88" N	44.65302°	00°	35' 24.97" E		0.59027°
					116 meters
11	◀ N	N21	35.6	1.0	**Castillonnès**
turn left on N21, D254 on right					
12	▶ SW	D416	36.6	8.8	**Castillonnès**
turn right on D416					
5% descent			**Montauriol** at 40.2 km		
13	▶ S	D241	45.4	5.0	
turn right on D241					
44° 34' 24.58" N	44.57349°	00°	34' 56.01" E		0.58223°
D206 on left at 46.0 km		D206 on right at 46.4 km			**148 meters**
14	▶ NW	D124	50.4	10.4	
turn right on D124, D256 straight ahead					
44° 32' 45.52" N	44.54598°	00°	32' 28.01" E		0.54111°
Monbahus at 51.0 km		D145 on right at 51.6 km			**143 meters**
D275 on right at 56.4 km			**Gardelle** at 60.2 km		
5% ascent			cross D667 at 60.4 km		
5% ascent					
			60.8	parking, **Tombebœuf**	

12 Buzet-sur-Baïse & Casteljaloux

Details:

Distance—72.2 kilometers

Climbing—430 meters

Challenge rank—4.5

Parking: at the Canal de Garonne marina near D12 in Buzet-sur-Baïse.

Bicycle southwest and west 5½ kilometers through Buzet and then north to Damazan. From Damazan ride 16½ kilometers west to Casteljaloux. Follow the route south 15¼ kilometers to Houeillès. From Houeillès cycle east 21¾ kilometers to Barbaste, then northeast 10½ kilometers along the Baïse Rivière through Lavardac, Vianne and Feugarolles to the Canal de Garonne. Finally, follow the cycle path northwest along the Canal de Garonne to Buzet-sur-Baïse.

There is one climb on the route. It starts at Villefranche-du-Queyran and gently climbs 105 meters in 4.0 kilometers.

Damazan

The Bastide de Damazan traces its foundation to 1259. It became a prize of the French and the British during the Hundred Years War rivalry. The village was repeatedly taken on several occasions and then suffered during later religious struggles.

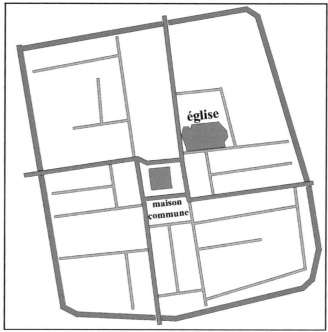

Bastide de Damazan Plan

The Bastide plan is the one generally followed in the thirteenth century: it forms a quadrangle around a

central location with a high main building called the *maison commune* (common house) and later expanded to be the *Hôtel de Ville* (City Hall). Around the *maison commune* on perpendicular streets, houses were built with the floor above the ground floor extending out from foundation and allowing a canopy for part of the ground floor.

Place Gambetta

The lower parts of these houses were built with stones and bricks. The upper floors used heavy frames forming the backbone of the building. The frames were made with local oak and chestnut trees. A mud mixture of earth and hay was used as fill between the rafters.

This walled and fortified village had only four entrance portals, one in each of the cardinal points. Alleys between houses ended in cul-de-sacs. Along the outside walls were wide defensive ditches.

Casteljaloux

The original importance of the town lies in it being part of the House of Albret from the eleventh to the fifteenth century. The origin of the town's development dates back to the eleventh century. In 1979, the charter of Casteljaloux was rediscovered in a pitiful state. The charter established the town and the right to build a church. It also set the rights of justice, the fees, specifies the privileges and grants a place for the monks to settle.

The layout of the medieval town dates back to this period. Fortifications surrounded the community. Some parts of the wall are still visible behind Notre Dame church or facing the Town Hall. At that time, three main gates allowed people to enter Casteljaloux.

During the thirteenth century, the Neuffonds springs, the presence of iron ore and the abundance of timber allowed establishment of iron forges, workshop for bronze bells and plates, paper mills, glassworks, tanneries and rope factories.

In 1550, the House of Albret was elevated to the status of duchy by Henri II. This act created four royal courts at Castelmoron d'Albret, Tartas, Nérac and

Casteljaloux. During this period, the town reached its peak and both the middle-class and legal professions appeared.

Also, the half-timbered houses date back to this era. They were built following the rules used in the region with a stone ground floor and a first floor with three superimposed wooden lines looking like a St-Andrew's cross. Additionally, they were decorated with ornamentation such as turrets or pinnacles. All these houses date back to the first half of the sixteenth century.

The Wars of Religion with the Protestants fighting against the Catholics broke out during this time of economic growth. In 1568, the Calvinists wreaked great havoc. They destroyed the Monastery of the Cordeliers and the Notre Dame church. The furniture and statues were also burned.

In 1636, Richelieu, under orders of the king, pulled down the walls and the advanced tower. In 1653, the donjon was demolished with the agreement of the residents who thus were discharged from paying the garrison. The Notre Dame church was rebuilt only in 1682 with the stones of the destroyed fortifications.

Place Gambetta in Casteljaloux

At the beginning of the nineteenth century, as a result of the general forestation of the region, Casteljaloux became an important center for trading and the conversion of forest products into resin, timber and turpentine.

The legend of the *charbonnier* (charcoal maker) Capchicot.

The area has a number of sites that conjure the memory of King Henri IV (1553 – 1610). Among them were the fortified Château Capchicot and the charcoal making facility. The attached forest was also a royal hunting preserve for the King of Navarre.

When staying in the region, the young Henry of Navarre (the future King Henri IV) enjoyed Casteljaloux and his passion for hunting.

One day, the king being lost, came at nightfall, knocked at the charbonnier's house and asked for hospitality. The charbonnier did not recognize his host (young Henry not being a friend on Facebook) and distrusted the visitor. Eventually he served Henry a

boar meat dinner and told him not to tell anyone because "Big Nose" (what was colloquially called the king) was very jealous of his hunting reserve.

The next morning at breakfast, Henry started a conversation about the privileges of the king. The charbonnier then complained that life was hard: the variable fee he had to pay every time he brought his charcoal to town, and the problem predicting when he might be rid of this tribute.

The charbonnier told Henry that he wanted to petition the king, but that he didn't know the procedure. The visitor then offered to take him to Durance where the king planned to be that day. The charbonnier agreed and both traveled on the same horse. Along the way, the charbonnier asked: "But how I would recognize the king?" Quite simply replied Henry, "you see, everyone is recognized before him, except he keeps his hair."

The crowd was already inside the Durance walls when the king, with his traveler, arrived in the middle of the small yard in an explosion of applause. "Well charbonnier" he said before dismounting, "do you now know the king?"

"By these absolute terms" the charbonnier replied without emotion, "but in this light, is it me or you that is King?" and, returning to his surprise, the charbonnier reminded him: "Well, do not forget the charcoal!"

A few days later, Henry received the charbonnier at the castle of Nérac and granted the privilege to sell charcoal exempt from all duties. The story even says that Henry granted him the fortified Château Capchicot that can still be seen today.

Barbaste

Moulin de Barbaste

The impressive Moulin de Barbaste stands beside the Gélise Rivière. It was built at the beginning of the fourteenth century and was the property of the House of d'Albret. The legend says that the four towers of the thirteenth century represent the four daughters of the miller. This was Jeanne d'Albret and his son Henry's (to become King Henry IV) estate. Perhaps first used as a tax collector's house, the mill evolved over the centuries becoming a fortress, mill, factory, and power plant.

Adjoining the mill is an exceptional twelfth century Romanesque, ten arch bridge that crosses the Gélise to the village.

Vianne

Initially, a hamlet was built around the ruins of a Roman villa. The Roman Ténarèse road passed through the present village.

The bastide of Vianne was founded on 21 September 1284 by an act signed by the Duke of Aquitaine as representative of King Edward I of England, while Philip III reigned over France. Actually in 1260, the French founded La Bastide de Lavardac upstream.

An Original Portal and Wall

The first fortifications of the new town (country house or villa nova) were built in the early fourteenth century, just before the beginning of the Hundred Years War (1337). They included a perimeter wall 1¼ kilometers long, four square towers and round towers. Construction began in 1284 and was completed in 1287. Vianne is most interesting because of its official plan, its gates and its walls, and well preserved houses. On an area of about ten hectares protected by walls, only a portion of the land was assigned to the first inhabitants. The gardens have always taken a lot of space. The general structure consisted of two roads: one, nearly 350 meters long from north to south and parallel to the Baïse Rivière, the other about 250 meters and perpendicular to the first. Other streets of different widths are parallel to each of these areas, but none of them led to a gate of the village.

During the Hundred Years War (1337 to 1453) the city was dotted with several skirmishes and battles between the French and the English. The first scuffle in Vianne

took place in 1295, even before the Hundred Years War. Lupiac Moncassin, whose son was killed, defended Vianne. The son's body was tied to the south gate and the English believed he was still alive, so they fought. Thereafter, Vianne passed to the French in 1337, taken back by the English in 1340, and again in 1342 the French took it, and so on until 1442 when it finally became French.

During the Wars of Religion the battle of Arrougets took place on 3 July 1562, a fight placed the "butcher of Catholics," one Captain Doazan, at the head of a 500 men army of Huguenots to stop Catholics. The battle was terrible, since Vianne had to bury more than 300 bodies, but saw the victory of the Catholics.

Under Henry IV, Vianne replaced the payssière (a crude sluice that permitted boats to navigate the rapids) with a manual lock operated by sailors. The lock was rebuilt to its current size in 1844, which allowed Vianne to accommodate larger vessels.

Under Louis XIV, in 1651, Vianne was ceded to the Duke of Bouillon, a foreign prince, which legalized it to be one of the few communities that did not destroy its fortifications.

Baïse Rivière Bridge Approach

More recent history of the town is written in its industry: stone quarries, corks and especially glassware, established in 1920. At the height of its activity nearly 900 workers manufactured glassware. The company was initially funded with Czechoslovak capital, and was accompanied by Czechoslovak immigration. Over the years, the glassworks were closed and reopened multiple times. Since May 2009, the furnaces were relit and glassware is again available to the public.

Moulin de Barbaste Detail

(Continued on page 50)

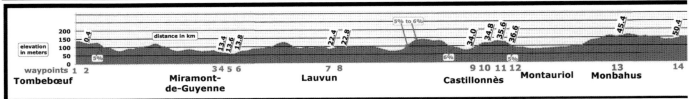

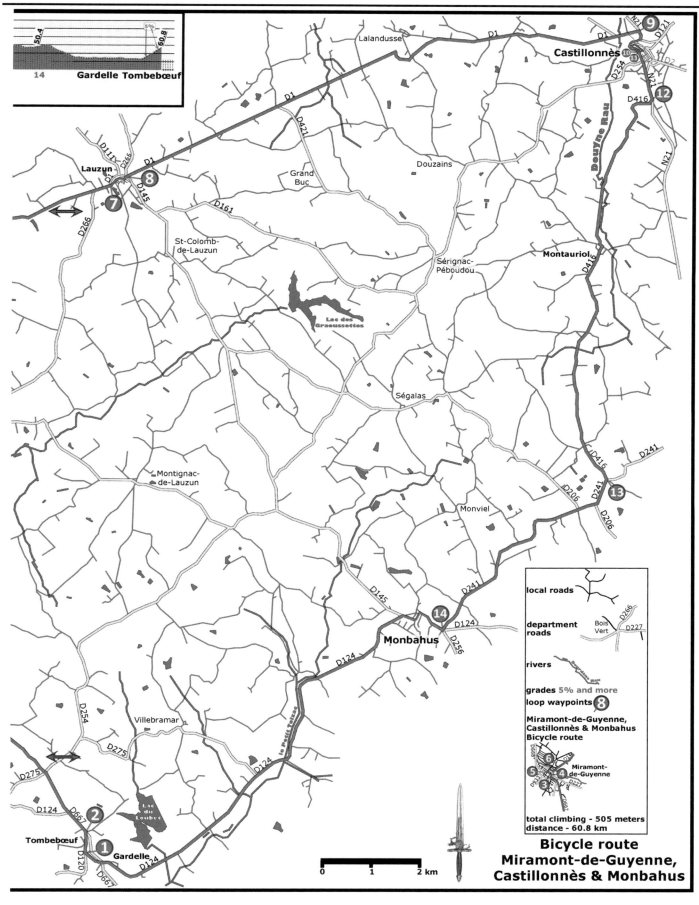

50.4   5%   60.8
14   **Gardelle Tombebœuf**

Lalandusse

Castillonnès

D1

D421

D111   D266   D1

Lauzun

D145

D266   D161

St-Colomb-
de-Lauzun

Grand
Buc

Douzains

Sérignac-
Péboudou

Montauriol

Lac des
Graoussettes

Ségalas

D416

D241

Montignac-
de-Lauzun

Monviel

D206   D241

D416

D206

D145

D241

Monbahus

D124

D256

Villebramar

D254

D275

D124   le Petit Vitrac

D275

D124   D667

Lac
du
Loubet

Tombebœuf

D124   D120   D667   Gardelle   D124

0   1   2 km

legend box:
local roads

department
roads   Bois
Vert   D266   D227

rivers

grades 5% and more
loop waypoints   8
Miramont-de-Guyenne,
Castillonnès & Monbahus
Bicycle route

Miramont-
de-Guyenne

total climbing - 505 meters
distance - 60.8 km

**Bicycle route
Miramont-de-Guyenne,
Castillonnès & Monbahus**

Queues and Directions

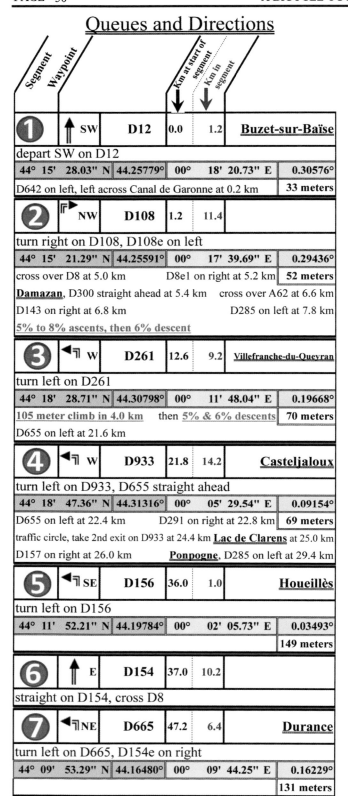

Segment	Waypoint			Km at start of segment	Km in segment	
①	↑ SW	D12		0.0	1.2	**Buzet-sur-Baïse**
depart SW on D12						
44° 15' 28.03" N	44.25779°	00°	18' 20.73" E			0.30576°
D642 on left, left across Canal de Garonne at 0.2 km						33 meters
②	⬏ NW	D108		1.2	11.4	
turn right on D108, D108e on left						
44° 15' 21.29" N	44.25591°	00°	17' 39.69" E			0.29436°
cross over D8 at 5.0 km D8e1 on right at 5.2 km						52 meters
Damazan, D300 straight ahead at 5.4 km cross over A62 at 6.6 km						
D143 on right at 6.8 km D285 on left at 7.8 km						
5% to 8% ascents, then 6% descent						
③	⬉ W	D261		12.6	9.2	Villefranche-du-Queyran
turn left on D261						
44° 18' 28.71" N	44.30798°	00°	11' 48.04" E			0.19668°
105 meter climb in 4.0 km then 5% & 6% descents						70 meters
D655 on left at 21.6 km						
④	⬉ W	D933		21.8	14.2	**Casteljaloux**
turn left on D933, D655 straight ahead						
44° 18' 47.36" N	44.31316°	00°	05' 29.54" E			0.09154°
D655 on left at 22.4 km D291 on right at 22.8 km						69 meters
traffic circle, take 2nd exit on D933 at 24.4 km **Lac de Clarens** at 25.0 km						
D157 on right at 26.0 km **Ponpogne**, D285 on left at 29.4 km						
⑤	⬉ SE	D156		36.0	1.0	**Houeillès**
turn left on D156						
44° 11' 52.21" N	44.19784°	00°	02' 05.73" E			0.03493°
						149 meters
⑥	↑ E	D154		37.0	10.2	
straight on D154, cross D8						
⑦	⬉ NE	D665		47.2	6.4	**Durance**
turn left on D665, D154e on right						
44° 09' 53.29" N	44.16480°	00°	09' 44.25" E			0.16229°
						131 meters
⑧	⬏ SE	D655		53.6	4.2	
turn right on D655						
44° 10' 56.95" N	44.18249°	00°	14' 10.87" E			0.23635°
Lusseignan at 55.2 km						91 meters
⑨	⬉ N	D642		57.8	4.4	**Barbaste**
turn left on D642, D109 on right						
44° 10' 12.22" N	44.17006°	00°	17' 11.21" E			0.28645°
cross Baïse Rivière at 58.0 km						56 meters
traffic circle, take 2nd exit on D642, D930 at 1st exit, at 58.4 km						
Lavandac, D258 on right at 59.2 km cross Baïse Rivière at 59.6 km						
D108 on left at 59.8 km cross under rail line at 61.8 km						
⑩	⬏ E	D642e		62.2	2.8	**Vianne**
turn right on D642e						
44° 11' 45.10" N	44.19586°	00°	18' 58.92" E			0.31637°
cross Baïse Rivière at 63.0 km						41 meters
⑪	⬉ N	D930		65.0	1.4	
turn left on D930						
44° 12' 36.10" N	44.21003°	00°	20' 21.67" E			0.33935°
						46 meters
⑫	⬉ N	D12		66.4	1.0	**Feugarolles**
turn left on D12						
44° 13' 19.38" N	44.22205°	00°	20' 48.89" E			0.34691°
cross D119 at 66.8 km cross under A62 at 67.2 km						53 meters
⑬	⬉ W			67.4	4.8	
turn left on path along S side of Canal de Garonne						
44° 13' 47.15" N	44.22976°	00°	20' 36.51" E			0.34348°
cross Baïse Rivière on Pont du Canal at 68.6 km						38 meters
cross right over canal to path along E side of Canal de Garonne at 69.0 km						
				72.2		**Buzet-sur-Baïse**
parking						

Durance South Portal

13 Agen, Canal de Garonne & Aiguillon

Details:

Distance—71.3 kilometers

Climbing—480 meters

Challenge rank—5.6

Parking: at the Canal de Garonne marina near D12 in Buzet-sur-Baïse.

Bicycle southeast and east 27¼ kilometers to Agen. Cycle through Agen and northwest 18¼ kilometers to Prayssas. Follow the route west 18½ kilometers to Aiguillon. From Aiguillon head south 7¼ kilometers to Buzet-sur-Baïse.

There are four short climbs on the route with ascents up to 6%, but no climb exceeds 100 meters.

Canal de Garonne

This canal was formerly known as Canal Latéral à la Garonne. It dates from the nineteenth century and connects Toulouse to Castets-en-Dorthe, 54 kilometers southwest of Bordeaux. The remainder of the route to Bordeaux uses the Garonne Rivière. It is the continuation of the Canal du Midi that connects the Mediterranean with Toulouse. Together they and the Garonne Rivière form the Canal des Deux Mers from the Mediterranean Sea to the Atlantic Ocean.

Canal Near Bruch

The canal skirts the northeast bank of the Garonne, crosses the river in Agen via the Agen aqueduct, and then continues along the southwest bank. It is connected to the Canal du Midi at its source in Toulouse, and emerges at Castets-en-Dorthe on the Garonne, a point where the river is navigable.

With the exception of the five locks at Montech, which are bypassed by the water slope, all of the locks have a length of 40.5 meters and a width of 6 meters.

Eighty-three bridges cross the canal. Most were rebuilt in 1933 to allow for the requirements of larger boats.

The canal is 18 meters wide. It is 193 kilometers long, has 53 locks and the Montech water slide. In total, it raises boats 128 meters.

The canal was inaugurated in 1856, but was considered a possibility since ancient times. Before the Canal du Midi was constructed, the passage between the Atlantic Ocean and the Mediterranean Sea was down the Spanish coast and through the Strait of Gibraltar, a 3,000-kilometer route with risks of attack and storms.

Nero, Augustus, Charlemagne, Francis I, Charles IX and Henry IV all wanted to construct a canal that avoided the detour. Their designers' problem was in supplying sufficient water at the watershed between the Mediterranean and the Atlantic to ensure continuous navigation.

Between 1614 and 1662, under the influence of Louis XIII and Louis XIV, five projects were proposed but none solved the water supply problem. Then in 1662 Pierre-Paul Riquet wanted to bring water to the place that would be the canal du Midi (between Toulouse and Sète) at a watershed near Seuil de Naurouze, where water flows both to the Mediterranean and the Atlantic. His knowledge of the Montagne Noire and its watercourses led him to envision a system based on the diversion of water from many streams and rivers.

Pont-canal sur la Baïse

This enabled the barges to cross the watershed, but they still had to use the Garonne to reach the ocean, and this presented more problems with floods and groundings as the size of cargo boats increased.

It is said that when Riquet built the Canal Royal du Languedoc (now known as the Canal du Midi) between Sète and Toulouse (1667-1681) he had the idea of continuing the canal closer to the Atlantic — the future Canal Latéral à la Garonne. However the successive enlargements of the Château de Versailles and the poor record of Louis XIV emptied the kingdom's coffers and the project never materialized. People had to be content with the navigation on the Garonne for two centuries.

A new route was surveyed, starting in 1828, and completed in 1830. However, it was only in 1832 that the state granted the concession in perpetuity to the private company, Magendie-Sion. There were delays due to disputes between the state and Magendie-Sion. A new act of 9 July 1835, set new construction dates. A third act in 1838 allocated a sum of 100,000 francs to the heirs of the Magendie-Sion founder and repurchased parts of the project for 150,000 francs. The project was then taken back into hand by the state with the divisionary inspector of Bridges and Roads in charge, and began in 1838 with a budget of forty million francs. Construction began at several points simultaneously with thousands of workmen building the 193 kilometers of canal and remarkable structures such as the famous Agen aqueduct.

Agen Aqueduct

In 1844, the section from Toulouse to Montech to Montauban was open. The canal was open for navigation to Buzet-sur-Baïse in 1853 and upstream by 1856.

The canal was completed at the same time as the Bordeaux to Sète railway that followed the same route. The first trains left Agen station in 1857.

In the beginning, the railway did not compete with water transport but later the state conceded the canal's exploitation rights to the *Compagnie de Chemin de Fer* (railway company) du Midi, the direct competitor of the boatmen. The railway company increased the levies on water transport. When the concession was

withdrawn in 1898 the damage was already done. Between 1850 and 1893, water freight diminished by two thirds.

However, until about 1970, the Canal Latéral à la Garonne was still mainly used with the transport of goods. In the years before 1970, the canal was upgraded to allow larger boats of the Freycinet gauge and to deal with increasing traffic on both the canals of the Canal des deux Mers. But it was a new kind of traffic that saved the canal: river and canal tourism.

After 1970, boats brought visitors to this exceptional site of natural and historical significance. In 1996 the canal du Midi was classified as a UNESCO world heritage site, which also benefited the connecting Canal de Garonne.

Buzet-sur-Baïse Marina

Now, nearly 1000 boats travel between the Mediterranean and Atlantic each year. The professional boat services include hotel boats, day and hourly tour boats and boat restaurants.

From 12 boats in 1970, the tourist fleet counts for 450 boats today and employs 500 people on a permanent basis.

Agen

From Neolithic times, the Garonne Rivière has defined Agen. Roads were almost non-existent when this was a Celtic community. Riverbanks, especially at the fords, were strategic areas both economically and militarily. During the Gallic Wars (58 to 50 Before the Common Era), the Garumna (from Garumnite, a tribe of the Spanish Pyrénées) mentioned by Julius Caesar was positioned as the boundary between peoples.

The region's economic role was demonstrated in the sixth century (Common Era) by a consul of the Emperor Gratian and by the geographers Strabo and Alboufeda when they wrote about minerals, skins, wool and wine being regularly transported between Bordeaux and Toulouse. From the Gallo-Roman period (first and second centuries) Agen was a commercial transit port through the river routes and became the second largest city of Aquitaine.

After the fall of the Roman Empire, the barbarian hordes overran the region, followed by the Normans in the ninth century. These invaders passed through Agen and used the waterway to go to Toulouse. It was during this period that the Garonne separated two peoples that evolved into two provinces and two Occitan dialects: the Languedoc to the north and Gascon to the south.

The irregularity of the river's course and violent floods forced the city to grow only on the right, or east bank. During the Middle Ages, four or five efforts to build a bridge linking the two sides failed, they were carried away with the regular floods. The first bridge worthy of the name to span the river was the Stone Bridge in 1827, replaced in 1972 by a vehicle bridge.

In the seventeenth century, the city imported from Bordeaux via the Garonne much more than it exported. From the Atlantic came sugar, spices and seafood, while it shipped local products consisting of tobacco, wine and flour.

Until the early twentieth century, the commercial vessels used were Miolles (reminds one of a long, flat-bottomed canoe) and barges, flat-bottomed boats with a shallow draft, about 20 meters long, suitable for low flow in the river. The boats' commercial docks numbered eleven in 1850; the river was competitive in terms of passenger transport. The link with Bordeaux took three days, twice as fast as by road.

But the Garonne had regular and devastating floods. These are deeply marked in the collective memory, especially the one of 1875, which reached a depth of 11¾ meters, and those of 1930 and 1956 that exceeded 10 meters.

Esplanade

The esplanade between the Garonne and Agen was originally an island and became, after drainage and landscaping, the meeting place of Agen society and an important place for the fair.

In the nineteenth century, Agen built the docks designed for ships carrying goods, passengers and gravel. But despite these achievements and the work of dredging the river, the esplanade remained an area regularly flooded. The bank was the object of

perpetual restructuring and towpaths had to be repaired after each disaster.

Place Jasmin

However, Agen skippers had competition from the railway since 1857, and had gradually abandoned the river, as it was no longer navigable. From the early 1880's, protection against floods becomes a political issue. Substantial and integrated site facilities today channel the Garonne with dikes along the banks such that a flood has not threatened the city center since 1930.

For barges to reach Bordeaux, boatmen left the Canal du Midi and went on the Garonne at Toulouse, which posed problems when use of the river was not feasible, imposing added costs for storage of goods and loss of time. In 1839 the government decided to start at several points with simultaneous construction of a canal link to the Atlantic. For seventeen years thousands of workers, armed with shovels and pickaxes, dug 211 kilometers of inland waterways, achieving remarkable works like the famous aqueduct bridge in Agen.

Prayssas

This pleasant village is unusual by its circular plan. The community was built around the old village church that occupies the site of a Gallo-Roman villa. Amanieu of Preyssas, one of four co-seigneurs, granted a charter in 1266. The town hall was built in the nineteenth century on the lower rooms of a grand château.

(Continued on page 56)

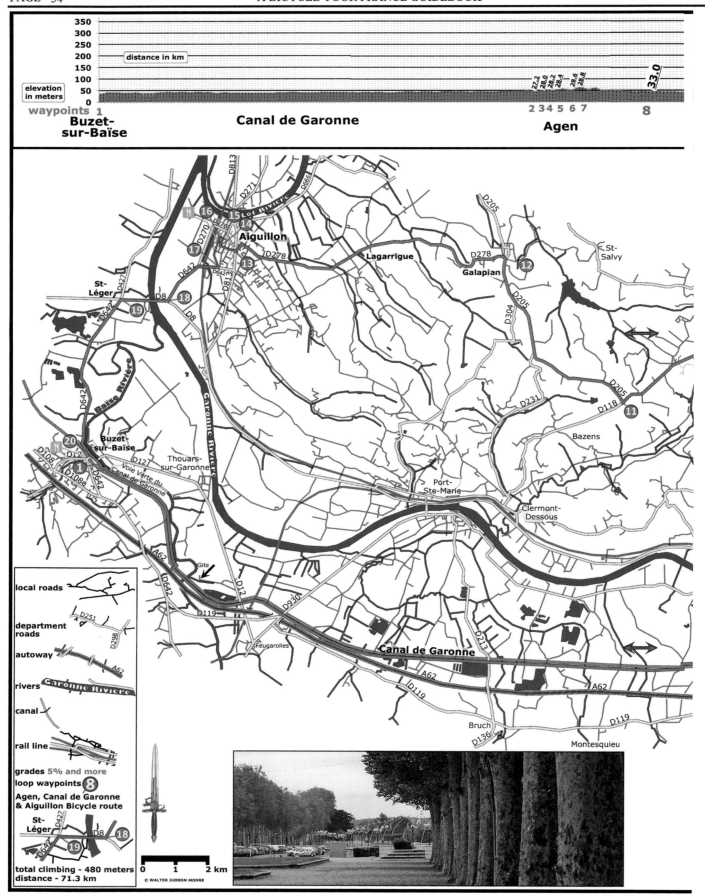

350
300
250
200
150
100
50
0

distance in km

elevation
in meters

27.2
28.0
28.2
28.4
28.6
28.8
33.0

waypoints 1   2 3 4 5 6 7   8

Buzet-sur-Baïse   **Canal de Garonne**   **Agen**

D813
D271
D661
D205
Lot Riviere
16 15 14
St-Salvy
D270
D270
Aiguillon
D278
Lagarrigue
D278
12
17
Galapian
13
D642
D278
D205
D304
St-Léger
D642
D81
D205
D8
18
D8
D642
19
D427
D231
D118
11
Baïse Riviere
Bazens
D642
Garonne Riviere
20
Buzet-sur-Baïse
D12
Thouars-sur-Garonne
1
D108
D108e
D12
Voie Verte du
Canal de Garonne
Port-Ste-Marie
Clermont-Dessous
A62
Gite
D642
D12
D119
D930
D213
Feugarolles
Canal de Garonne
A62
A62
D119
Bruch
D119
D136
Montesquieu

Legend:

local roads

department roads   D251   D298

autoway   A62

rivers   Garonne Riviere

canal

rail line

grades 5% and more
loop waypoints 8
Agen, Canal de Garonne & Aiguillon Bicycle route

St-Léger
D427
D8 18
D642
19

total climbing - 480 meters
distance - 71.3 km

0   1   2 km
© WALTER JUDSON MOORE

6% to 7%

5% to 6%

5% to 6%

5% to 6%

5% to 6%

45.4
45.8

52.4

57.0

63.4
63.8
64.0
64.1
64.8
66.2
67.2
71.2
71.3

5% to 7%

5% to 7%

5%

5%

5% to 6%

Lusignan-Petit

9 10

Prayssas Frégimont

11

12

Galapian

13 14 15 16 17 18 19

Aiguillon

St-Léger

20

Buzet-sur-Baïse

**Bicycle route
Agen, Canal de Garonne
& Aiguillon route**

Many stone houses are gathered close in two concentric circles around the center and church. The Église of St-John the Baptist has Romanesque and Gothic parts. It was reconstructed following the destruction caused by the Wars of Religion in 1569.

Église of St. John the Baptist

In the nineteenth century, the church spire was struck by lightning and replaced with the current spire. Near the church are a number half-timbered sixteenth century houses.

Two and a half kilometers east of the village in the Masse Valley is Néguenou Lake. Throughout the Masse Valley are old watermills that provided the supply of flour to the surrounding population.

Queues and Directions

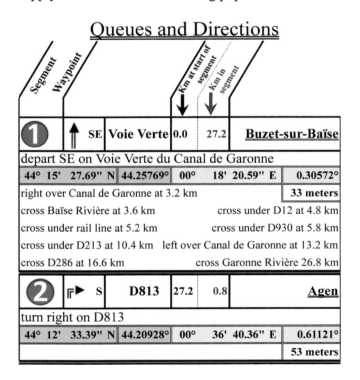

				Km at start of segment	Km in segment	
①	↑ SE	Voie Verte		0.0	27.2	**Buzet-sur-Baïse**

depart SE on Voie Verte du Canal de Garonne

44° 15' 27.69" N	44.25769°	00°	18' 20.59" E	0.30572°
right over Canal de Garonne at 3.2 km				**33 meters**

cross Baïse Rivière at 3.6 km   cross under D12 at 4.8 km

cross under rail line at 5.2 km   cross under D930 at 5.8 km

cross under D213 at 10.4 km   left over Canal de Garonne at 13.2 km

cross D286 at 16.6 km   cross Garonne Rivière 26.8 km

②	⬏ S	D813	27.2	0.8	**Agen**

turn right on D813

44° 12' 33.39" N	44.20928°	00°	36' 40.36" E	0.61121°
				53 meters

③	◀⬑ E		28.0	0.2	**Agen**

turn left on Rue Lomet

④	◀⬑ NE		28.2	0.2	**Agen**

turn left on Rue Richard Cœur de Lion

⑤	◀⬑ N		28.4	0.2	**Agen**

turn left on Rue Voltaire

⑥	◀⬑ W		28.6	0.1	**Agen**

turn left on Boulevard de la République

⑦	🔄▶ N	D813	28.7	4.3	**Agen**

traffic circle, take 1st exit on D813

44° 12' 15.90" N	44.20442°	00°	36' 43.43" E	0.61206°
cross over Canal de Garonne at 29.2 km				**49 meters**

D302 on right at 29.8 km   D418 on right at 30.4 km

cross rail line at 30.6 km

traffic circle, 2nd exit on D813, N1021 on 1st exit at 32.2 km

D215 on right at 32.6 km

⑧	⬏ NW	D107	33.0	12.4	

turn right on D107

44° 13' 20.24" N	44.22229°	00°	34' 07.61" E	0.56878°
cross rail line at 34.4 km				**42 meters**

5% to 6% ascents, then 5% to 7% descents, followed by 5% to 6% ascents

Lusignan-Petit, D245 on left, D245 on right at 41.4 km

5% to 7% descents, followed by 5% to 6% ascents

⑨	⬏ E	D107e	45.4	0.4	**Prayssas**

turn right on D107e

44° 17' 13.66" N	44.28713°	00°	30' 29.01" E	0.50806°
				171 meters

⑩	↑ SW	D118	45.8	6.6	

straight on D118   *5% descent*

44° 17' 18.17" N	44.28838°	00°	30' 32.85" E	0.50913°
D280 on right at 46.6 km D298 on right at 49.0 km				**172 meters**

Frégimont at 51.0 km

⑪	⬏ NW	D205	52.4	4.6	

turn right on D205

44° 17' 09.65" N	44.28601°	00°	26' 39.31" E	0.44425°
D231 on left at 54.8 km D304 on left at 56.0 km				**184 meters**

No.	Dir	Road	km	dist	Destination
12	◄↰NW	D278	57.0	6.4	**Galapian**
turn left on D278					5% to 6% descents
44° 17' 50.89" N	44.29747°	00°	24' 48.32" E		0.41342°
					133 meters
13	↑ W		63.4	0.4	**Aiguillon**
cross over D813, straight on Rue Verdun					
44° 17' 56.70" N	44.29908°	00°	20' 32.16" E		0.34227°
					45 meters
14	↱ N		63.8	0.2	**Aiguillon**
turn right on Cours Alsace et Lorraine					
15	◄↰ W		64.0	0.1	**Aiguillon**
turn left on Place 14 Juillet					
16	◄↰ S		64.1	0.7	**Aiguillon**
turn left on Rue Thiers, becomes Rue Victor Hugo					
17	↱ W	D642	64.8	1.4	
turn right on D642					
44° 17' 44.60" N	44.29572°	00°	20' 17.24" E		0.33812°
cross rail line at 65.0 km					42 meters
18	↱ W	D8	66.2	1.0	
turn right on D8					
44° 17' 21.77" N	44.28938°	00°	19' 26.93" E		0.32415°
cross Garonne Rivière, **St-Léger** at 66.4 km					31 meters
19	◄↰SW	D642	67.2	4.0	
turn left on D642					
44° 17' 22.92" N	44.28970°	00°	18' 42.76" E		0.31188°
					31 meters
20	↑ SE	D12	71.2	0.1	**Buzet-sur-Baïse**
straight on D12					
44° 15' 31.06" N	44.25863°	00°	18' 13.98" E		0.30388°
					36 meters
			71.3	parking, **Buzet-sur-Baïse**	

Prayssas View

Marina Camping Near Buzet-sur-Baïse

14 Buzet-sur-Baïse, Nérac & Francescas

Details:

Distance—70.6 kilometers

Climbing—445 meters

Challenge rank—4.9

Parking: at the Canal de Garonne marina near D12 in Buzet-sur-Baïse.

Bicycle south 19½ kilometers through Feugarolles, Vianne and Lavardac to Nérac. From Nérac ride 12 kilometers southeast to Francescas. Follow the route north 22 kilometers through Sérignac-sur-Garonne to the Voie Verte du Canal de Garonne. Finally, follow the cycle path west along the Canal de Garonne to Buzet-sur-Baïse.

There is one climb on the route. It starts just before the right turn on D7 (**waypoint 22**) climbing 115 meters in 3.0 kilometers with 5% to 7% ascents.

Buzet-sur-Baïse

Buzet Marina

The village is four kilometers from the confluence of the Baïse and Garonne rivers in the heart of the Middle Garonne area of the Aquitaine basin. Its 2,115 hectares spreads over three portions: the terrace with the village, the hill to the west which overlooks the village and is either forested or planted with vines, and the flood plain to the east of the Baïse and Garonne.

The soil of the terrace and the slope is very suitable for growing grapevines, while in the plain to the east fruit, vegetables and corn are cultivated. The climate is soft and moist with Mediterranean summers.

Buzet has been occupied since prehistoric periods. In the Roman era, farms were spread on the terrace. In the Middle Ages, a village grew up around the château on a rocky spur overlooking the valley. There were probably several aristocrats who each had a building. At the end of the Middle Ages, there was only one nobleman who modernized the château by adding the two towers and another staircase tower on the south facade. The Château de Buzet is private property. As

of June 2013, this 500 square meter, 14-room château was listed for sale.

The Buzequais developed a new hotel in 1838, a rectory in 1858, and a church that was consecrated in 1862. Digging the Canal de Garonne, which opened in 1856, somewhat changed the landscape of Buzet, but largely resulted in the development of commercial activities with the already significant Baïse Rivière.

According to archival documents, the main activity has always been agriculture, predominantly viticulture.

There was also intense milling activity along the local creeks. After World War I, the largest mill was converted into a pencil factory lending some notoriety to Buzet throughout France during the inter-war years and into the 1950s. It went out of business in the early 1960s.

Buzet is now well known thanks to the Cave des Vignerons that was started in the 1950s by a handful of growers who wanted to free themselves from the demands of wine merchants. It is a commercial and quality success.

On 22 June 1944, the Nazi SS stationed at Château de Buzet executed six patriots. They also killed five other people between 22 June and 13 July. In April, they had arrested three members of a family of farmers and their employee suspected of aiding The Resistance, the son was killed trying to escape. He jumped into the Garonne Rivière during transfer to a jail, was strafed and then found drowned. The other three disappeared in exile.

Nérac

Château of King Henri IV

A stroll through Nérac is a walk through the history of Aquitaine. Research implies human occupation from the Bronze Age in the area. However, it is the Romans who left the best evidence, as with the fourth-century villa, with its mosaics still visible today, at the entrance of the park or on the interior walls of City Hall.

A document from the Benedictine abbaye of Condom in 1088 is regarded as the founding record of the community. This led to the construction of a fortified town with a market, then a priory, and the building of churches St-Nicolas and St-Michel. From 1310 to 1440, the city's development included the building of a second line of walls and fortified gates. In 1306, the Albret region got complete jurisdiction of Nérac. Weddings and acquisitions allowed Albret to become one of the first lineages of the kingdom, heirs to the crown of Navarre, and then France.

Baïse Rivière Through Nérac

An important page in the history of France was written here. Jeanne d'Albret required the protestant Calvinist doctrine to be followed. Jeanne d'Albret's son, Henri III of Navarre, the future Henry IV of France, had then political prominence. He spent part of his youth in Nérac where he established his reputation as a "The Green Gallant". Henry was nicknamed Henry the Great (*Henri le Grand*), and in France he is also called *le bon roi Henri* ("the good king Henry") or *le vert galant* ("The Green Gallant").

Nérac became home to the Accounts Chamber in1527 and the Chamber of the Edict of Guyenne in 1598, and then the capital of the duchy of Albret. From 1578 to 1579, Catherine de Medici came to negotiate peace during the Conferences of Nérac.

After the glory of the Renaissance, Nérac stalled in the seventeenth century. This, at the time, Protestant community surrendered to the royal army in 1621, and many important buildings were destroyed. Institutions were transferred to Bordeaux and Pau. Then in the eighteenth century, Nérac returned to prosperity as a result of its leather tanneries, mills and the flour trade to the Caribbean. During The Revolution, three of the four wings of the château were destroyed.

During the nineteenth century, the community leaders encouraged development of the railway. In the late nineteenth and throughout the first half of the twentieth, industrial activity improved with several metallurgical plants, two breweries, shoe and sandal factories and a pasta factory.

l'Église Notre Dame

Also, over the centuries, it became the epicenter of Armagnac, the oldest brandy in France, and culinary specialties like duck confit, foie gras, duck rillettes, roasted pigeon and pie flamed with Armagnac.

Francescas

In the eleventh century, Francescas belonged to the Abbaye of Gourdon. As with most communities in France of the Middle Ages, the village peasants (who were bound to the land) held tenant holdings from a lord or monastery (for which they paid rent). In 1161, this church and town are listed among the goods of the abbaye of Condom. The construction of the village was prior to the walled towns of Agen, which dates from the twelfth and thirteenth centuries. In 1369, Charles V of France offered Francescas to the Comte d'Armagnac.

Etienne de Vignolles, called La Hire, (Born 1390 - died 11 January 1443) was a French military commander during the Hundred Years War. He fought alongside Joan of Arc in the campaigns of 1429. He owned a house in Francescas, which is now a small hotel and upscale restaurant.

In the latter part of the sixteenth century, the settlement was enclosed by a strong fortification, surrounded by moats, and was entered by four portals. From mid-sixteenth century up to 1621, the Francescas inhabitants supported religious struggles, and therefore the walls were constantly being repaired. Streets were paved during the middle of the seventeenth century. In the years 1770 through 1780, the fortifications that no longer served the population were demolished. In the eighteenth and nineteenth centuries, the village was extended north and east.

(Continued on page 62)

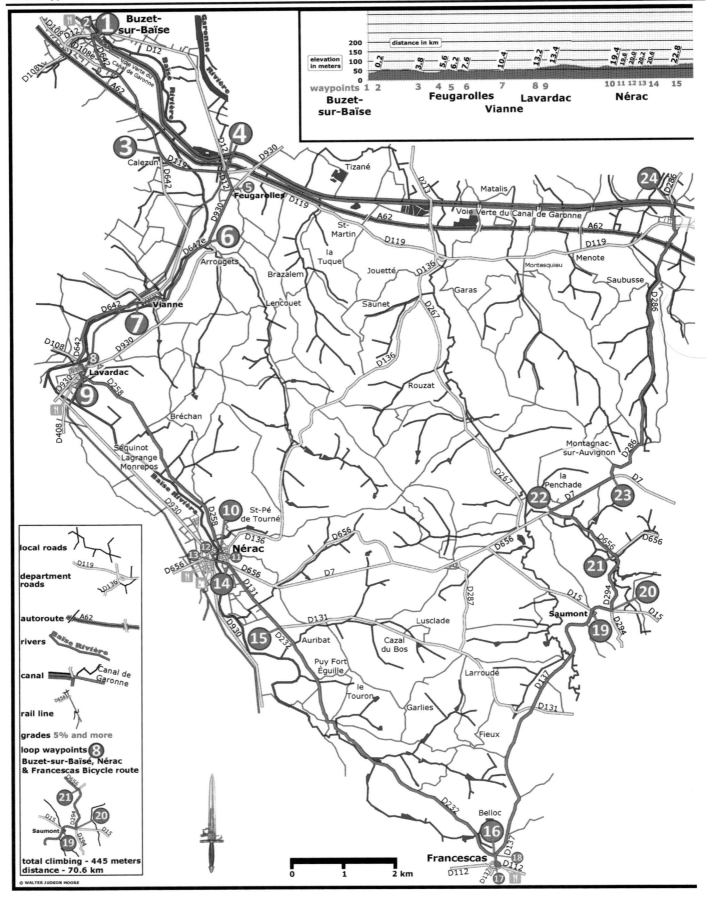

Buzet-
sur-Baïse

distance in km

elevation
in meters

200
150
100
50
0

0.2
3.8
5.6
6.2
7.6
10.4
13.2
13.4
19.4
19.6
20.0
20.2
20.6
22.8

waypoints 1 2   3   4 5 6   7   8 9   10 11 12 13 14   15

Buzet-
sur-Baïse
Feugarolles
Vianne
Lavardac
Nérac

Calezun
Tizané
Matalis
Voie Verte du Canal de Garonne
Feugarolles
St-
Martin
la
Tuque
Brazalem
Jouetté
Montesquieu
Menote
Saubusse
Arrougets
Lencouet
Saunet
Garas
Vianne
Rouzat
Lavardac
Bréchan
Montagnac-
sur-Auvignon
Séquinot
Lagrange
Monrepos
la
Penchade
St-Pé
de Tourné
Nérac
Lusclade
Auribat
Cazal
du Bos
Larroudé
Puy Fort
Éguille
le
Touron
Garlies
Fieux
Saumont
Belloc
Francescas

local roads

department
roads

autoroute

rivers

canal

rail line

grades 5% and more

loop waypoints

Buzet-sur-Baïsé, Nérac
& Francescas Bicycle route

total climbing - 445 meters
distance - 70.6 km

© WALTER JUDSON MOORE

0   1   2 km

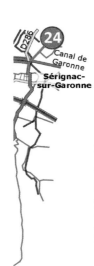

**Bicycle route
Buzet-sur-Baïse,
Nérac & Francescas**

Typical Village Market Square

Sérignac-sur-Garonne

The village owes its name to the Gallo-Roman landowner Serenius who had a large property 75 kilometers east along the Garonne Rivière. Archaeological remains from the early years of the Christian era including pottery shards, coins, fragments of tiles and bricks were found in the town.

The walls of the fortified village collapsed at the end of the sixteenth century. However, the medieval character is still visible today with timbered houses and narrow streets.

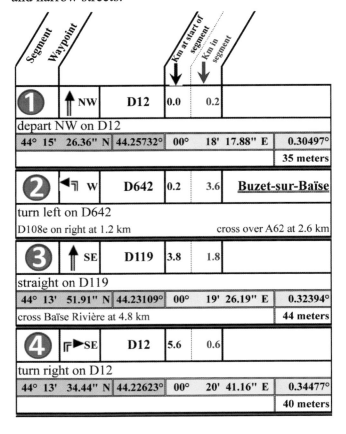

Segment	Waypoint		Road	Km at start of segment	Km in segment	
1	↑ NW		D12	0.0	0.2	
depart NW on D12						
44° 15' 26.36" N	44.25732°	00°	18' 17.88" E			0.30497°
						35 meters
2	◀↰ W		D642	0.2	3.6	**Buzet-sur-Baïse**
turn left on D642						
D108e on right at 1.2 km				cross over A62 at 2.6 km		
3	↑ SE		D119	3.8	1.8	
straight on D119						
44° 13' 51.91" N	44.23109°	00°	19' 26.19" E			0.32394°
cross Baïse Rivière at 4.8 km						44 meters
4	⇱▶SE		D12	5.6	0.6	
turn right on D12						
44° 13' 34.44" N	44.22623°	00°	20' 41.16" E			0.34477°
						40 meters
5	⇱▶SW		D930	6.2	1.4	**Feugarolles**
turn right on D930						
44° 13' 18.88" N	44.22191°	00°	20' 48.32" E			0.34676°
						52 meters
6	⇱▶SW		D642e	7.6	2.8	
turn right on D642e						
44° 12' 36.03" N	44.21001°	00°	20' 21.38" E			0.33927°
cross Baïse Rivière at 9.6 km, becomes D141						47 meters
Vianne at 9.8 km						
7	◀↰ W		D642	10.4	2.8	
turn left on D642						
44° 11' 45.17" N	44.19588°	00°	18' 58.57" E			0.31627°
cross under rail line at 10.6 km						42 meters
cross Baïse Rivière at 12.8 km				**Lavardac** at 13.0 km		
8	⇱▶ W		D930	13.2	0.2	**Lavardac**
turn right on D930						
44° 10' 46.04" N	44.17946°	00°	17' 52.12" E			0.29781°
						56 meters
9	◀↰ SE		D 258	13.4	6.0	**Lavardac**
turn left on D258				cross rail line at 13.6 km		
10	↑ S			19.4	0.2	**Nérac**
straight on Rue Gaujac						
44° 08' 16.75" N	44.13799°	00°	20' 32.34" E			0.34232°
						59 meters
11	⇱▶ W			19.6	0.4	**Nérac**
turn right on Rue Sully				becomes Rue Pusoque		
12	◀↰ S			20.0	0.2	**Nérac**
turn left on Cours Romas						
13	◀↰ SE		D656	20.2	0.4	**Nérac**
turn left on D656				cross Baïse Rivière at 20.4 km		
14	⇱▶ SE		D131	20.6	2.2	**Nérac**
turn right on D131						
44° 08' 02.91" N	44.13414°	00°	20' 42.09" E			0.34503°
						61 meters
15	↑ SE		D232	22.8	8.4	
straight on D232						
44° 07' 10.12" N	44.11948°	00°	21' 37.96" E			0.36054°
5% ascent						63 meters

BORDEAUX & the PYRÉNÉES   PAGE 63

---

16 ☞ S | D137 | 31.2 | 0.4 |
right on D137 through Francescas
44° 03' 57.62" N | 44.06601° | 00° 25' 42.67" E | 0.42852°
130 meters

17 ◄ E | D112 | 31.6 | 0.2 | **Francescas**
turn left on D112

18 ☞ N | D137 | 31.8 | 7.8 |
turn right on D137   D232 on left at 32.0 km
5% descent, then 5% ascent

19 ☞ NE | D15 | 39.6 | 0.6 | **Saumont**
turn right on D15
44° 07' 23.38" N | 44.12316° | 00° 27' 32.02" E | 0.45889°
5% descent   133 meters

20 ◄ N | D294 | 40.2 | 1.6 |
turn left on D294
44° 07' 22.51" N | 44.12292° | 00° 27' 53.69" E | 0.46491°
99 meters

21 ◄ NW | D656 | 41.8 | 2.2 |
turn left on D656
44° 08' 09.92" N | 44.13609° | 00° 27' 58.98" E | 0.46638°
115 meter ascent in 3.0 km   70 meters

22 ☞ NE | D7 | 44.0 | 1.8 |
turn right on D7
44° 08' 57.50" N | 44.14931° | 00° 27' 16.39" E | 0.45455°
5% to 7% ascents   68 meters

23 ◄ NW | D286 | 45.8 | 8.0 |
turn left on D286
44° 09' 15.97" N | 44.15444° | 00° 27' 57.55" E | 0.46599°
cross over A62 at 52.6 km   cross D119 at 53.2 km | 170 meters
Sérignac-sur-Garonne at 53.4 km

24 ◄ W | | 53.8 | 16.8 |
turn left on Voie Verte du Canal de Garonne
44° 13' 03.99" N | 44.21778° | 00° 29' 06.08" E | 0.48502°
cross under D930 at 64.6 km   43 meters
cross under rail line at 65.2 km   cross under D12 at 65.6 km
cross over Baïse Rivière at 67.0 km

70.6 parking, **Buzet-sur-baïse**

Baïse Rivière Marina at Lavardac

Vianne Bridge

15 Villeneuve-sur-Lot & Lot Rivière

Details:

Distance—67.7 kilometers

Climbing—175 meters

Challenge rank—3.9

Parking: at the lot near D666e and D146 in Lafitte-sur-Lot.

Bicycle northeast and south of the Lot Rivière 29 kilometers into Villeneuve-sur-Lot. From Villeneuve-sur-Lot cycle southwest and close to the north bank of the Lot Rivière 25 kilometers to Roussanes. After crossing the Lot Rivière, ride southwest 3 kilometers to parking in Lafitte-sur-Lot.

The route is nearly flat with only a few bumps.

Lot Rivière

The Lot rises on the southern slope of the Montagne du Goulet in Lozère department from an approximate altitude of 1,300 meters, flows 485 kilometers, growing into a large waterway as it joins the Garonne at Aiguillon in the Lot-et-Garonne department.

Lot Rivière at Casseneuil

It is mainly fed by rain, which explains the low flow in the fall and the spring floods. The watershed of the river is 10,700 square kilometers. A typical flow at Villeneuve-sur-Lot is 151 cubic meters per second. The maximum daily flow recorded was 2,450 cubic meters per second on 4 December 1976.

Prior to the establishment of railways, the Lot was a very important commercial waterway. Since 1991, as a result of a series of projects, the river is again navigable for boaters on two sections, from the Garonne to Lustrac in the Lot-et-Garonne department, and from Luzech to Larnagol in the Lot department. Added projects are planned and funded.

Eleven dams were established in the late thirteenth century and paid for by the King of England. Some locks were built under Colbert in the seventeenth century; other works are part of a recent series that date to the nineteenth century.

Ste-Livrade-sur-Lot

As with most of the Lot and Garonne valleys, man has occupied the area of the village from early antiquity, and predominantly since the first Iron Age. It was built as a bastide in 1289.

The Occitan name of Santa Liorada d'Olt disappeared with the conquest of Occitan by the Albigensian Crusade (1209 through 1229, a military campaign initiated by Pope Innocent III to eliminate Catharism, a Christian movement that challenged the Catholic church in the south of France) and with the Edict of Villers-Cotterêts in 1539, which imposed the French language. As a result Santa Liorada d'Olt became St-Livrade-d'Agenais or St-Livrade. In December 1919, to differentiate two or three other regional hamlets and villages also named St-Livrade, the French government imposed the name of Ste-Livrade-sur-Lot.

The community became a multicultural city with Italians, Spaniards and Portuguese fleeing poverty or fascism throughout the middle of the twentieth century. French Indochinese arrived in 1956 at the end of the Indochina War when French soldiers and armed auxiliaries left Vietnam.

More French soldiers and Algerian auxiliaries arrived in 1962 and 1963 at the end of the war in Algeria. France's open border policy with Algeria allowed migrants to settle in Ste-Livrade, and the rest of France, in the latter part of the twentieth century.

Tour du Roy

This monument was built in the late thirteenth and early fourteenth centuries, and is all that remains of a fortified château. The tower was converted into a prison during The Revolution. Its imposing and austere exterior staircase leads to the first floor room of vaulted brick arches. Currently, temporary exhibitions are held on three levels.

Villeneuve-sur-Lot

This ancient bastide has now largely given way to a much larger town that surrounds it.

A fortified wall with six towers and eight gates once surrounded Villeneuve-sur-Lot. The center of the town is between two of these old gateways, the Porte de Paris and the Porte de Pujols, which are easily spotted as you approach the town from either direction.

Rue de Pujols With Porte de Pujols

The Porte de Paris was built in the fourteenth century and like Villeneuve itself is a mixture of stone and red bricks. The third floor of the tower at one time was the prison and the fourth floor had a walkway that could serve as a high lookout point.

In the town center, there are now real shops (not tourist shops). Cycle down the Rue de Paris, the main street between the two towers and the main shopping street of Villeneuve-sur-Lot, and on to the Place Lafayette. Place Lafayette, surrounded by arcaded shops, is the town main square.

The morning markets are held on Tuesday and Saturday at the Covered Market Hall just down from the Place Lafayette on the river. The market hall was built in 1864 of cast iron and stone in a similar style to those in Paris.

On Rue Ste-Catherine behind the Place Lafayette is Église Ste-Catherine. A fairly unique structure, it is built from red bricks with an elaborate tower. This Romano-Byzantine style church was started in the nineteenth century and finished in 1937.

At the river, there are three bridges that cross the Lot. The bridge you cycled over is the *Pont Vieux* (old bridge), a thirteenth century bridge based on the bridge at Cahors, but it has lost its original towers.

The Embankment From Pont Vieux

On the other side of the river is a small medieval-style garden and the Chapelle des Pénitents Blancs, the chapel of the white penitents. The members practiced collective penitence and carried out work for the poor and sick of the local area.

Other points of interest in the town are the Gajac Mill which has been converted into the Art Museum of Villeneuve-sur-Lot; the Saint Cyr Hospital, a beautiful building donated to the town and which still has its original nineteenth century pharmacy with 500 decorated porcelain pots.

Casseneuil

A great fear was the grassroots movement that took place in France from 20 July to 4 August 1789. According to some, there was a rumor that an aristocratic conspiracy would arm bandits to ravage crops and ruin the peasants. For others it would be a revolution intended to arm the cities.

At 18:00 on Thursday, 30 July a man came riding in from Montastruc announcing that enemy British troops the were burning the village of Eymet and had taken possession of Lauzun. The population began to worry and was ordered to patrol at night. The next day all was quiet and the rumor was forgotten.

But the panic had an unintended consequence: the peasants and the people were able to arm themselves quickly without waiting for an order from the lords and priests.

On 29 September 1789, the date payment of rents were due in kind to the lords, a rumor spread in Cancon that feudal rights had been abolished and that rent did not need to be paid. Vicomte de Beaumont, Lord of the baronies of Cancon and Casseneuil received a memorandum written by Monsieur Cadot of Argeneuil, "To put an end to the murmurs of the people, it is proposed to either pay the rent on the original title dated from the year 1500, or to retain the pension [keep the rent money] until new regulations by the National Assembly." In response, the Vicomte replied firmly that this was not inadmissible and "the duty of the Committee Cancon was to ensure the execution of decrees, not to infringe upon ... I only have the means of laws and I would put it in use."

Thirteenth Century Église St-Pierre and St-Paul

Meanwhile, the Casseneuillois (people of Casseneuil) continued to worry. On 12 October, a portion of the population, led by Costes, harangued the crowd to lead a revolt against the Standing Committee. The local assembly met to appoint municipal officers. On the last Sunday in November in Cancon, Madam Chauvet and Madam Auzeral threated to demolish the attic of the Lord and hang those who did pay rent.

In January 1790, at the request of Monsieur Cadot, the Vicomte agreed to cancel a decree against Chauvet and Auzeral but demanded in return a letter of repentance and the immediate payment of rent.

On 31 January 1790 at the end of the Mass, it was decided to bring weapons into Casseneuil to force the Vicomte into canceling the decree, but the Standing Committee hesitated. On 2 February 1790, Cancon received reinforcements from Lougratte and revolted. The attic of the Lord was plundered. But Vicomte de Beaumont, in his château near the church of Casseneuil, refused to give in. He was not a man to be intimidated. This was the signal for the revolt.

On 3 February 1790, angry farmers from Cancon and its surroundings began to besiege Casseneuil. The crowd swelled as it progressed toward Casseneuil and the Vicomte's château. At 15:00 they were 1,200 strong when they arrived at the gates of Casseneuil to face Vicomte de Beaumont, owner of the Barony of Cancon and Casseneuil. They demanded the release of Madam Chauvet and Madam Auzeral, along with the suspension of the payment of pensions

Monsieur Cadot of Argeneuil took command of this crowd.

The Standing Committee of Casseneuil, reinforced by confederates from Ste-Livrade and Villeneuve-sur-Lot, sent a detachment to meet the crowd.

The Vicomte de Beaumont finally gave in after receiving Monsieur Cadot and a deputation of eleven leaders of his troop.

The case could have ended without bloodshed, but gentlemen had come to support Vicomte de Beaumont.

Some of these supporters of the Vicomte followed the crowd to monitor their actions, thinking they would run off with their tails between their legs. The Vicomte's supporters were annoyed to see the crowd leave proudly, and happy to have been able to bend the Vicomte. The Vicomte's supporters decided to pursue them and give them a "good thrashing."

Most of these farmers, to run faster, left their shoes. Only five or six of the less agile were caught.

Those that were caught received a good fly green wood (whipping with a green stick).

By decree of the National Assembly dated 15 January 1790, Casseneuil became head of the local canton. This changed in 1800 when Casseneuil was attached to Cancon.

I sure am pleased to observe that local politics has changed so much.

Castelmoron-sur-Lot

In the thirteenth century, a number of families were located near a swamp and around a château along the river. It was called Castelmoron in 1259. Villages established at this time were normally bastides, but Castelmoron did not benefit from this custom: it was probably a castrum (a rudimentary military camp or small fort) as per a 1259 tax report.

Street Scene

At the beginning of the Hundred Years War in 1345, the village was taken by the British troops of the Earl of Derby. The Earl gave it to the Chevalier de Caumont, who was at the scene. In 1435, the French retook it and its fortifications were dismantled.

In the sixteenth century, it joined the Calvinists of Agen. That reformed church was founded in 1559. The community was spared during the Wars of Religion through a 1609 agreement between Catholics and Protestants, however, the temple, initially prohibited, was torn down in 1693.

The revocation of the Edict of Nantes (18 October 1685) caused a number of Protestants to leave France. Mathieu Maury, a person raised in Castelmoron, left for America. His descendants distinguished themselves in the founding of the United States, including his son James, a school principal who counted among his pupils Thomas Jefferson, future president of the United States.

During the eighteenth century, there were two major floods that destroyed part of the Moulin de Lacoste (dating from 1290) and Moulin Neuf (from the early eighteenth century). This was also the height of river navigation on the Lot Rivière. Many barges starting at the Castelmoron port carried wine and flour to Bordeaux for the countries of northern Europe and the French Antilles. A trade flow was established with Santo Domingo and Louisiana led by masters of Castelmoron vessels. Some also settled in the Antilles. At the end of the eighteenth century, the loss of the American colonies finally closed the trading horizon.

Halle

The village went through The Revolution without damage. However, Jacques Bujac of Castelmoron was guillotined at Bordeaux on 21 December 1793 for his contacts with the Gironde party. At the beginning of the First Empire, another local became famous for his courage and daring. On 12 April 1805, Pierre Alexandre Marauld Dupon, commander of the privateer Retaliation, beat and put to flight the Santander, an English schooner of far superior strength. Dupon earned the nickname Agen Corsair.

In 1845, to allow the provincial road 13 through Castelmoron, a suspension bridge was built over the Lot at the site of the thirteenth century church, which was torn down.

The replacement church was built on the site of the former cemetery in 1852. The old château was purchased in 1871 by the widow of Felix Solar and was completely transformed according to his designs drawn before his death 1870. He was a native of Castelmoron and son of a Portuguese family that came to Castelmoron after the revolutions of Santo Domingo.

The municipality purchased Château Solar in 1902 to become the Mairie (town hall). Solar also gave Castelmoron the fountain with water jets built in 1859 on the site near the halle (market place).

In 1875, on the site of the old ferry dock, an imposing stone quay was constructed. Unfortunately, the river

traffic was declining despite the enormous work done both on the Garonne and Lot including improved locks and towpaths, and construction of quays. Competition from rail and the development of the road network gave a blow to commercial navigation on the river that finally ended in 1923.

Villeneuve-sur-Lot Waterfront

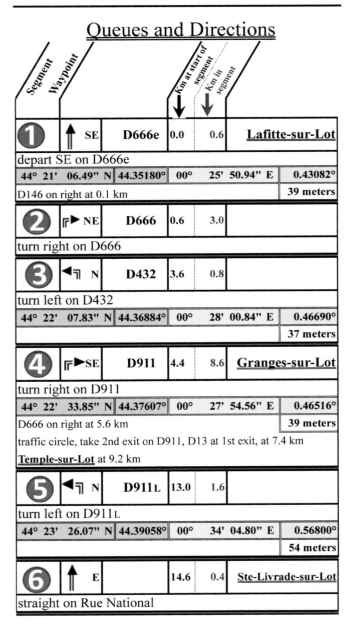

Queues and Directions

Segment	Waypoint			Km at start of segment	Km in segment	
①	↑ SE	D666e	0.0	0.6	**Lafitte-sur-Lot**	
depart SE on D666e						
44° 21' 06.49" N	44.35180°	00°	25' 50.94" E		0.43082°	
D146 on right at 0.1 km					39 meters	
②	⇨ NE	D666	0.6	3.0		
turn right on D666						
③	⇤ N	D432	3.6	0.8		
turn left on D432						
44° 22' 07.83" N	44.36884°	00°	28' 00.84" E		0.46690°	
					37 meters	
④	⇨ SE	D911	4.4	8.6	**Granges-sur-Lot**	
turn right on D911						
44° 22' 33.85" N	44.37607°	00°	27' 54.56" E		0.46516°	
D666 on right at 5.6 km					39 meters	
traffic circle, take 2nd exit on D911, D13 at 1st exit, at 7.4 km						
Temple-sur-Lot at 9.2 km						
⑤	⇤ N	D911L	13.0	1.6		
turn left on D911L						
44° 23' 26.07" N	44.39058°	00°	34' 04.80" E		0.56800°	
					54 meters	
⑥	↑ E		14.6	0.4	**Ste-Livrade-sur-Lot**	
straight on Rue National						

(Waypoints continued on page 70)

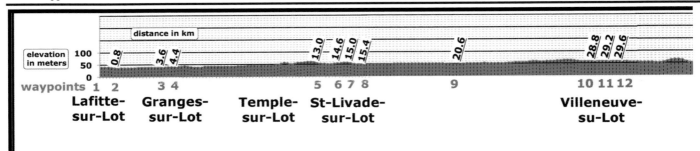

© WALTER JUDSON MOORE

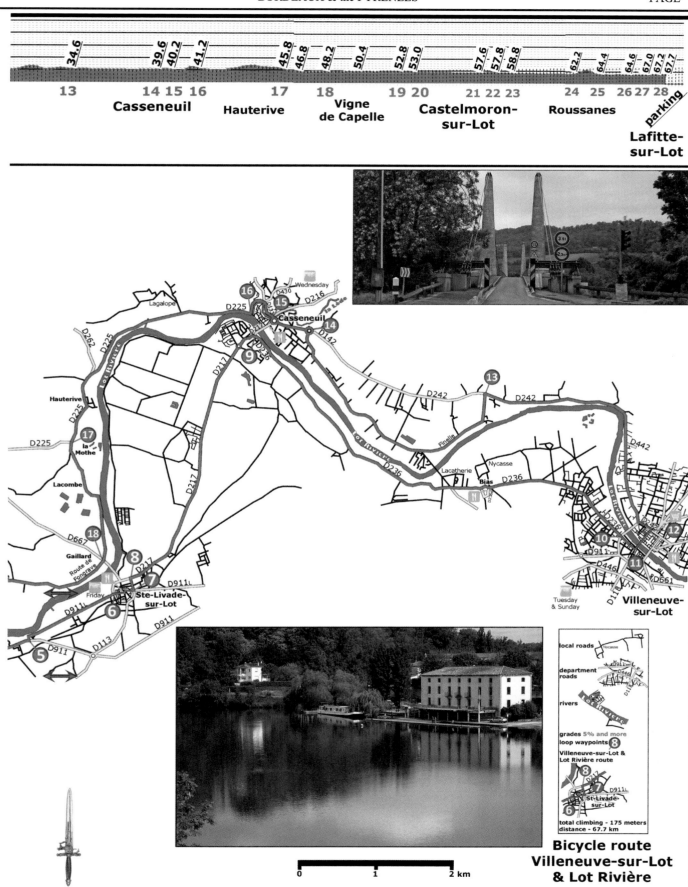

34.6 39.6 40.2 41.2 45.8 46.8 48.2 50.4 52.8 53.0 57.6 57.8 58.8 62.2 64.4 64.6 67.0 67.2 67.7

13   14 15 16   17   18   19 20   21 22 23   24 25 26 27 28
     Casseneuil   **Hauterive**   **Vigne**   **Castelmoron-**   **Roussanes**   *parking*
                                     de Capelle   **sur-Lot**
                                                                                            Lafitte-
                                                                                            sur-Lot

Lagalope
Wednesday
D430 D216
D225 la Lède
Casseneuil
Hauterive
D262 D225 Lot Rivière
D225
Hauterive
D217
D225 D242
la Mothe D225 Finelle
D217 Lacatherie Nycasse
Lacombe D236 Bias D236
D667 Lot Rivière D442
Gaillard D217 D911 **Villeneuve-**
Route de Fondrave D217 **sur-Lot**
Friday D911L D911L D446 D661
Ste-Livade- D118
sur-Lot D911 Tuesday
D911 & Sunday
D113
D911

0   1   2 km

local roads Nycasse
department roads D911L D446
rivers Lot Rivière
grades 5% and more
loop waypoints ⑧
Villeneuve-sur-Lot &
Lot Rivière route
⑧ D217
⑦ D911L
St-Livade-
sur-Lot
⑥
total climbing - 175 meters
distance - 67.7 km

Bicycle route
Villeneuve-sur-Lot
& Lot Rivière

7 ◀●N | D911L | 15.0 | 0.4 | Ste-Livrade-sur-Lot
traffic circle, take 4th exit on D911L

8 ▶E | D217 | 15.4 | 5.2 | Ste-Livrade-sur-Lot
turn right on D217   traffic circle, take 2nd exit on D217 at 20.2 km

9 ▶SE | D236 | 20.6 | 8.2
turn right on D236
44° 26' 27.83" N | 44.44106° | 00° | 37' 04.24" E | 0.61784°
traffic circle, take 2nd exit on D236 at 25.6 km | 48 meters
through **Bias**, traffic circle, take 3rd exit at 26.0 km

10 ↕SE | 28.8 | 0.4 | Villeneuve-sur-Lot
traffic circle, take 2nd exit on Rue St-Étienne
44° 24' 27.22" N | 44.40756° | 00° | 41' 58.14" E | 0.69948° | 57 meters

11 ◀NE | 29.2 | 0.4 | Villeneuve-sur-Lot
turn left, cross Pont des Cieutats, becomes Rue des Cieutats

12 ◀NW | D242 | 29.6 | 5.0 | Villeneuve-sur-Lot
turn left on D242   traffic circle, take 1st exit on D242 at 30.0 km

13 ◀S | 34.6 | 5.0
turn left toward Finelle
44° 25' 52.77" N | 44.43133° | 00° | 40' 09.82" E | 0.66939°
continue toward Cassenuil at 35.2 km | 55 meters
traffic circle, take 1st exit toward Cassenuil at 36.4 km

14 ◀●W | D242 | 39.6 | 0.6 | Cassenuil
traffic circle, take 4th exit on D242
44° 26' 30.67" N | 44.44185° | 00° | 37' 48.51" E | 0.63014° | 53 meters

15 ●▶NW | D133 | 40.2 | 1.0 | Cassenuil
traffic circle, take 1st exit on D133   D216 on right at 40.4 km
traffic circle, take 3rd exit on D133, D430 on 1st exit, D273 on 2nd exit, at 40.6 km

16 ▶W | D225 | 41.2 | 4.6
turn right on D225
44° 26' 40.17" N | 44.44449° | 00° | 37' 01.98" E | 0.61722°
D262 on right at 44.4 km | **Hauterive** at 45.0 km | 60 meters

17 ◀S | 45.8 | 2.4
turn left toward la Mothe
44° 25' 23.93" N | 44.42331° | 00° | 34' 38.22" E | 0.57728°
la Mothe, stay left toward Lacomb at 46.0 km | 59 meters
Lacombe, continue along Lot Rivière at 46.8 km

18 ↑SW | 48.2 | 4.6
cross D667, straight on Route du Fongrave
44° 24' 12.95" N | 44.40360° | 00° | 35' 05.25" E | 0.58479°
Vigne de Capelle at 50.4 km | 47 meters

19 ◀S | 52.8 | 0.2
turn left on D238, make 1st left toward Fongrave
44° 23' 47.15" N | 44.39643° | 00° | 32' 01.95" E | 0.53388° | 45 meters

20 ▶SW | 53.0 | 4.6
turn right along Lot Rivière
44° 23' 40.73" N | 44.39465° | 00° | 32' 06.56" E | 0.53516° | 46 meters

21 ◀NW ▶ | 57.6 | 0.2 | Castelmoron-sur-Lot
turn left on D13, turn right on Rue Gabriel
44° 23' 47.80" N | 44.39661° | 00° | 29' 40.56" E | 0.49460° | 41 meters

22 ◀SW | D249 | 57.8 | 1.0 | Castelmoron-sur-Lot
turn left on D249

23 ◀S | 58.8 | 3.4
turn left along Lot Rivière

24 ◀SW | D249 | 62.2 | 2.2
turn left on D249
44° 23' 07.44" N | 44.38540° | 00° | 27' 26.31" E | 0.45731° | 39 meters

25 ◀SE | D911 | 64.4 | 0.2
turn left on D911, cross Lot Rivière
44° 22' 25.74" N | 44.37382° | 00° | 26' 14.25" E | 0.43729° | 34 meters

26 ↑SE | 64.6 | 2.4
straight toward Lafitte-sur-Lot

27 ▶SW | D666 | 67.0 | 0.2
turn right on D666
44° 21' 12.53" N | 44.35348° | 00° | 25' 40.06" E | 0.42779° | 36 meters

28 ◀●E | D666e | 67.2 | 0.5
traffic circle, take 3rd exit on D666e, D146e at 1st exit, D666 at 2nd exit

67.7 | parking, **Lafitte-sur-Lot**

16 Monein, Navarrenx & Mourenx

Details:

Distance—41.4 kilometers

Climbing—580 meters

Challenge rank—6.1

Parking: at the Mairie parking lot in Monein.

Bicycle west 18½ kilometers to Navarrenx. From Navarrenx, cycle 15 kilometers northeast to Mourenx. Follow the route southeast 7 kilometers to Monein.

There are many climbs on the route. However, there is only one climb at 100 meters. It starts as the route crosses D109 and climbs 100 meters in 2.4 kilometers with 5% to 8% ascents.

Monein and St-Girons

The historic church of St-Girons in Monein is the largest Gothic church built in Béarn region.

Église St-Girons

The construction of the church began on 13 July 1464, when Gaston IV of Béarn and King Louis XI reigned in France. It took fifty years and was funded primarily by the taxes that the community imposed and paid during the period, along with gifts and bequests of clergy and local nobles.

The length of the nave is 50 meters. The bell tower is a square with sides of 6 meters. The width of the structure at the base is 16 meters. The walls and buttresses are 1¼ to 1½ meters thick.

It is a flamboyant Gothic style with Renaissance elements. Its construction was completed in 1520.

St-Girons Interior

Surprisingly, the actual St-Girons was a Vandal. In late December 406 of the Common Era, the Germanic Alans and Suevi Vandal tribes crossed the frozen Rhine near Mainz and invaded the Roman Empire. They assaulted Gaul and plundered for two years without encountering significant resistance. In 409, they entered Spain and then occupied most of North Africa in 429.

St-Girons arrived with the invaders. He converted to Christianity and received baptism from the hands of Sever (later St-Sever), also originally a Vandal. Along with five other converts, they traveled to Rome and were received by Pope Innocent I between 401 and 417. They were charged by the Pope to preach to and convert people of Aquitaine. While in the Aquitaine, they received the news of the death of Sever their father in faith. He was killed during a clash between people of the city where he was bishop and a band of Vandals. Girons and his companions traveled to Sever's city and gave him a Christian burial. Vandals set on them, Girons was seriously injured and he died some six months later.

In a niche of the church is a reliquary containing the relics of St-Girons.

A remarkable point of this church is the asymmetry of the building. A single aisle flanks the main nave. The unit interior architectural elements and large common framework suggest that this does not result from an accident during construction, but it was on the original plan.

The actual furniture dates from the seventeenth and eighteenth centuries; it replaced the original and cult objects that disappeared during the Reformation.

The original altar was sent to Rome just prior to a Protestant takeover during the Hundred Years Wars. The organ was built by Toulouse organ builder Sir Robert Delaunay starting in April 1683, and finished the following year. The instrument has been restored at least three times, the latest in 1972.

Roof Support Structure Sketch

A stone spiral staircase leads to the roof structure which is a very remarkable part of the building, and quite unique in France. The roof construction, not visible from the nave, is designed as an asymmetrical overturned dual-hulled vessel. It was built in heart oak, hand shaped with axes. It looks like a forest and took a thousand oaks to build it. This construction sits on walls 14 meters above the ground. The ridgeline is 32 meters above the ground. All of the oak structure is joined without any nails.

During spring, summer and fall, you may visit the roof area Tuesdays through Saturdays during the afternoons.

The church bell tower has a height of 40 meters with half-meter thick walls and is supported by large buttresses.

Navarrenx

Wedged between France and Spain, the independent Vicomte de Béarn occupied an unenviable position at the beginning of the sixteenth century. In addition, in 1521, the Lords of Béarn were weakened in a vain attempt to recapture the Spanish Navarre they had inherited from the King.

In 1469, Francis Phoebus ascended the throne of Navarre and became Lord of Béarn. But in 1512, the Castilian troops invaded Navarre and seized Pamplona after a blitz of five days, forcing the sister of Francis Phoebus, Catherine and her husband Jean d'Albret, who had become the sovereigns following the death of Francis Phoebus, to take refuge on the other side of the Pyrénées. Despite the support of the King of France, who had made an attempt to recapture the territory, the year ended with a failure. In 1521, their son, Henry II of Albret, mounted an expedition to reclaim part of his kingdom located beyond the Pyrénées. Again there was failure, resulting in the temporary loss of the Lower Navarre.

Two years later, in retaliation, the Spanish, commanded by the Prince of Orange, invaded Béarn and ransacked the main cities that were poorly defended by obsolete fortifications.

Henry II, Vicomte de Béarn decided to secure his position strengthening Navarrenx using modern principles of the time. The geographical location of Navarrenx alone justified his choice.

Although the medieval fortifications of Navarrenx were minor and very dilapidated, their existence is certain. The King of Navarre decided to bolster the Navarrenx fortifications and make them safe from new gunpowder (smooth bore) artillery.

At the end of the fifteenth century, the community suddenly found that medieval fortifications were unable to withstand a new weapon, gunpowder artillery.

From the beginning of the sixteenth century, many conflicts shook their countries. It was the Italian architects' methods that changed the design of fortifications. Departing from the designs that used medieval towers and stonewalls; they invented what would become the bastion with pentagonal, clay-coated masonry and projections from the enclosure. An example was the new Italian fortress of Civitavecchia. A new wall that eliminated blind spots in front of the buildings used a pentagonal shaped stronghold that surrounded the town.

Building of the Navarrenx fortifications started in March 1538 when the lords met in Pau and allocated a large sum of money to finance the construction, with a subsequent challenge by the Parliament of Bordeaux, which had complained to the King of France to denounce the threat to Navarrenx. But Francis I said that this is nothing more than the "power [struggle] between two monkeys." Of little consequence for France, the place could indeed serve as an outpost against Spain and defend the French border cheaply.

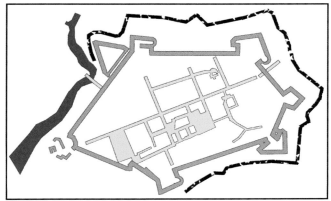

Fortification Plan of 1766

This work was significant at the time, as many populated areas were demolished under the wall foundations.

On 29 April 1546, Navarrenx received its first military governor, who promised to "well and faithfully guard the city, and the newly built Navarrenx fortress." The walls were built in less than nine years. On 20 July 1549, a new governor hired a master mason and instructed him to build a parapet 2⅓ meters thick. These dimensions are those of the existing building. It took less than twelve years for Henri II d'Albret to realize his fortress.

South Demi-Bastion

The walls consist of earth fill with alternating layers with rough-cut blocks between the two stone walls. They are 10 meters high, a wide base and a truncated apex supporting a walkway protected by a 2⅓-meter thick parapet.

The walls enclose an area about 390 meters in length and 253 meters in width; a 1,657-meter perimeter consisting of cut yellowish sandstone blocks.

Few changes have been made to the original appearance of the fortified wall.

The city also had an artillery foundry near the church.

In the first half of the nineteenth century, several studies concluded the need for change as a result of rifled artillery. Navarrenx was finally decommissioned as a military site in 1868, and its garrison was removed.

The role of Navarrenx in the centuries that followed the annexation of Béarn to France declined to the point of the total dismantling of the walls in the middle of the twentieth century. Today, thanks to the combined efforts of many, the city still offers a magnificent example of the first steps of the bastion. It was only the appearance of rifled artillery that made it obsolete. With the gradual restoration of all military construction, Navarrenx offers an exceptional example of military architecture of the period.

Mourenx

In 1951, a large discovery of natural gas was made 6½ kilometers north of Mourenx at Lacq. A large industrial complex was built. The complex produces sulfur from hydrogen sulfide, electricity, aluminum, gasoline, propane, butane, and ethylene.

In the early 1960s the French Ministry of Reconstruction planned and authorized construction of a completely new city, Mourenx, primarily for the Lacq employees. The plan and subsequent realization consists of a core center with a square, the town hall, shopping center, public services and a church; four and five story apartment buildings; subdivisions with town houses and individual homes in the periphery and in the hills; schools, shops, cultural and sports facilities, two office buildings for the professions; and with separation between pedestrian and automobile traffic.

Typical Downtown in Mourenx

In 1999, the population was 658. By 2011, the population grew to 7,583. There is a visually agreeable, landscaped parkway as you enter the town. It does take some perseverance to locate a place to eat.

Compared to other communities of similar or smaller size in the Aquitaine Region, Mourenx lacks the charm expected. Perhaps that will come with maturity, but that will be difficult with its backdrop of apartment boxes.

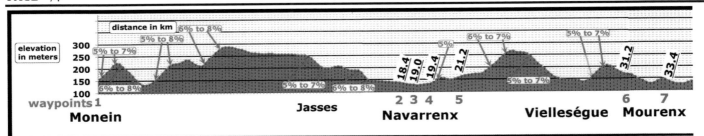

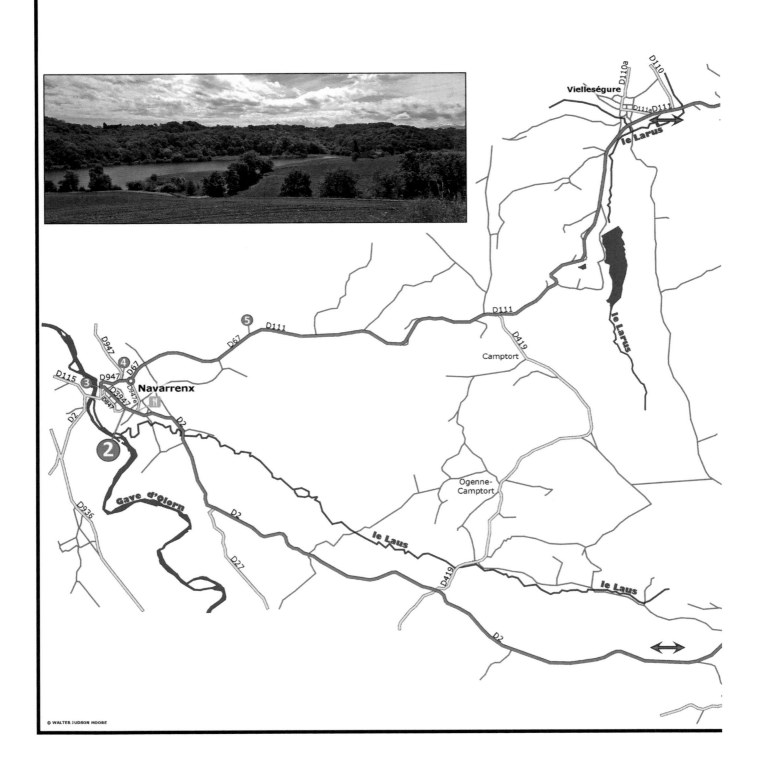

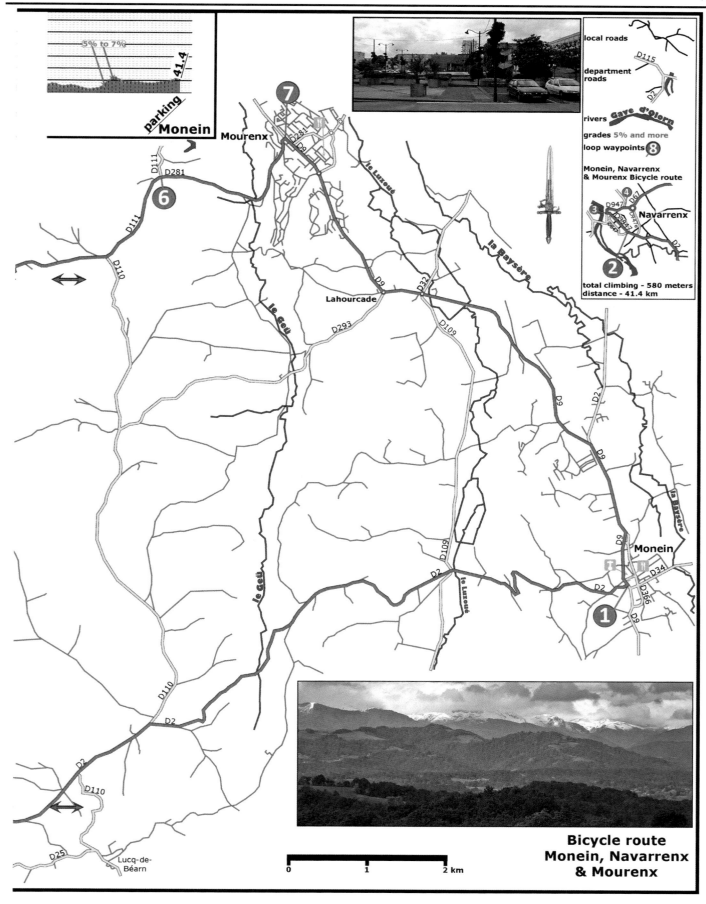

parking
Monein

5% to 7%
41.4

Mourenx

D281
D9

D111
D281

6

D111

D110

Monein

local roads

department
roads

D115
D2

rivers Gave d'oloron

grades 5% and more

loop waypoints 8

Monein, Navarrenx
& Mourenx Bicycle route

4 D67
3 D947
D947 Navarrenx
D947
D947

2

total climbing – 580 meters
distance – 41.4 km

7

le Luzoué

la Baysère

le Geü

Lahourcade

D9 D32

D293

D109

D9

D2

D9

D109

le Luzoué

D2

Monein

D9 D34
D2 D366
D9

1

D110

D2

D2

D110

D25

Lucq-de-
Béarn

0   1   2 km

**Bicycle route
Monein, Navarrenx
& Mourenx**

Queues and Directions

Segment	Waypoint			Km at start of segment	Km in segment	
①	↑ SW	D2	0.0	18.4		**Monein**
depart SW on D2					5% to 7% ascent	
43° 19' 11.94" N	43.31998°	00°	34' 44.62" W			-0.57906°
6% to 8% descents		cross D109 at 2.8 km				157 meters
100 meter ascent in 2.4 km					5% to 8% ascent	
D110 on right at 7.8 km			D110 on left at 9.0 km			
5% to 7% descents			cross D419 at 13.6 km			
6% to 8% descents			D27 on left at 16.6 km			
Jasses at 16.8 km						
②	↑ NW	D3947	18.4	0.6		**Navarrenx**
straight on D3947						
43° 19' 14.67" N	43.32074°	00°	45' 29.47" W			-0.75819°
						129 meters
③	⇒► N	D947	19.0	0.4		**Navarrenx**
turn right on D947						
④	↑ E	D67	19.4	1.8		
straight on D67		traffic circle, take 2nd exit on D67 at 19.6 km				
5% ascent						
⑤	↑ E	D111	21.2	10.0		
straight on D111					6% to 7% ascents	
D419 on right at 24.6 km					5% to 7% descents	
Villeségure at 28.0 km			D111a on left at 28.4 km			
D110 on left at 28.6 km			D110 on right at 30.0 km			
⑥	↑ E	D281	31.2	2.2		
straight on D281						
43° 22' 02.72" N	43.36742°	00°	39' 05.93" W			-0.65165°
						172 meters
⑦	⇒► SE	D9	33.4	8.0		**Mourenx**
turn right on D9						
43° 22' 19.32" N	43.37203°	00°	37' 57.38" W			-0.63261°
traffic circle, take 2nd exit on D9 at 34.0 km						133 meters
D293 on right at 35.8 km						
traffic circle, take 2nd exit on D9, D109 at 1st exit at 36.4 km						
5% to 7% ascent			D2 on left at 39.4 km			
D366 on left at 40.8 km			**Monein** at 41.0 km			
			41.4			**parking, Monein**

Navarrenx Businesses

Monein Mairie Parking

Sheep

17 Pau/Jurançon, Gan & Monein

Béarn Pyrénées View

Details:

Distance—68.4 kilometers

Climbing—885 meters

Challenge rank—7.6

Parking: Jurançon at the corner of Rue Charles de Gaulle and Avenue Charles Touzet.

Bicycle east through Jurançon then south to Gan. Follow the hilly route west to D9 and north to Monein. From Monein cycle east and follow the Gave de Pau to parking in Jurançon.

There are three climbs of note on this route. The first starts just west of Gan and climbs 145 meters in 4.6 kilometers with 5% to 7% ascents. The second starts west of Lasseube and climbs 135 meters in 5.4 kilometers with 5% to 7% ascents. The last climb starts in Monein and ascends 125 meters in a short 1.8 kilometers with 5% to 9% ascents.

Béarn

This region around Pau is first documented as a Viscounty in the ninth century. In the thirteenth century, the English occupied Béarn, as part of Gascony. They fortified many of the towns in the Béarn during the fourteenth century. The remains of these fortifications can be seen at Orthez, Pau and Sauveterre-de-Béarn.

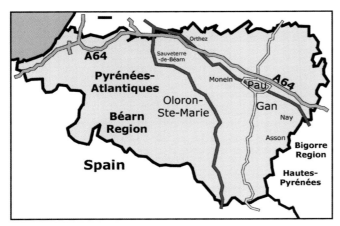

King Philip IV of France confiscated Béarn and Bigorre in 1292. The area was surrendered to Edward III of England in the 1360 Treaty of Brétigny, which ended the first phase of the Hundred Years' War. Recaptured by the French and their allies between 1370 and 1406, Bigorre was granted by King Charles VII of France to the Count of Foix in 1426.

Later, the House of Foix-Béarn passed through heiresses to the House of Albret, and then eventually to the House of Bourbon with Henry III of Navarre. Henry III of Navarre became King Henry IV of France in 1589. In 1607, he united the area to the French crown.

During the Napoleonic wars, Wellington's army passed through the Béarn, winning an important battle at Orthez and setting up a garrison at Pau. The British were very well received in the area and many soldiers from Wellington's campaign set up home in the Béarn when they retired.

The geography of the Béarn is dominated by the valleys of the two large mountain river sources (called *Gaves* locally): the Gave d'Oloron and the Gave de Pau—two of Europe's finest salmon and trout fishing rivers.

Pau

In the fourteenth century, the Count of Foix refused to pay tribute to the Black Prince. The English were threatening as they took Lourdes and Bayonne. A great captain expanded the outposts on the Béarn borders. Around 1370, the small wooden fort at Pau was enlarged to include a brick fortress and dungeon. With its renovated walls and five towers, the fortress was admired by the lord of Caumont who stated "This is the most beautiful castle (in) the world····. If, in my opinion, this is the best I aye seen and best of all things complicated." The Italian Renaissance gradually penetrated into France. Young Gaston IV of Foix was recognized for his education and culture. He hated the dark houses and implemented a large remodel for the Pau Château. Large openings were included; the height of the château was increased and roofed with slate. On 14 September 1464, he made Pau, with a population of less than 2,000, the capital of Béarn.

In the following century, the ancient fortress housed the Lords of Navarre. Henri d'Albret married Margaret, sister of King of France, François I. The small château did not suit this famous Queen. She added more stone, illuminated facades and ancient medallions. The gardens became among the most notable in Europe. The house was now ready for the birth of Henry IV, the king most popular in the history of France.

Whereas Henri IV gave the town its nobility, Napoleon told of dazzling horizons and a romantic landscape. Pau's reputation was built on an imperial look and grew thanks to Britons who loved its climate.

Pau welcomed the Republic with little violence. The local government voted against the death of King Louis XVI. The people of Béarn hailed new ideas, but they did not want bloodshed. Business took over the city, fortunes were made and the mayor compensated a climate of speculation with free education for the poor and an office of Charity and Orphanage.

With Napoleon the First, the city took a positive step with the creation of a route from Paris to Madrid via Pau, thus opening the Pyrénées' landscape to travelers.

In July 1808, upon returning from installing his brother Joseph on the Spanish throne, Napoleon stopped in Pau. He judged that: "The city is as poor as any, the castle is in ruins but what wonderful scenery!"

The eighteenth century established "a holy horror in the mountains." Madame de Maintenon, undeclared and controversial second wife of King Louis XIV, accompanied the ailing Duke of Maine on a trip to Barèges. On the way, they crossed the Col de Tourmalet. In one of three letters written to King Louis she wrote, "this place is all frightful gorges and peaks—the kingdom of Satan." The steward Le Bret reported it was "regrettable to find the presence of these high mountains that block the view."

Accompanied by Josephine, Napoleon was struck by the Pau Château and had the walls that encircle the Place Royale pulled down. He then established decisive decrees that trace the paths of future development in this town by creating a road from Paris to Pau, Madrid and Zaragoza. The decrees instigated installation of the town hall in the building of Notre-Dame and transferred the prisons in the dungeon of the Hôtel Gassion.

The first balloon flights to take place at Pau happened in 1844. The "aeronauts" brightened the winter seasons with their flights in "lighter than air" craft. The Wright Brothers left Le Mans in December 1908 with their model A Flyer. They settled near Pont-Long, Pau in January 1909. The Wright Brothers made their first flight from there on 3 February 1909. The Wright brothers opened an aviation school with two students, which were completing their training started in Le Mans.

Until 1914, Pau had the only seven aircraft manufacturers in the world and became the world capital of aviation.

The French Military Aviation School, *École Militaire de Pau*, moved there in 1911, and formed the fighter aces school for France in WWI. It trained more than 6,000 combat pilots between 1914 and 1918. This resulted in the celebrated Lafayette Escadrille.

Gan

Gaston II de Foix-Béarn established this village as a bastide in 1335. The village plan includes perpendicular axes around a large square. An embankment, a wooden fence and two parallel channels separated by twenty meters, surrounded the square. Three stone portals equipped with harrows provided entry to the bastide. The North portal, dating from the late fourteenth century, remains. A market is held in the central square on Wednesday mornings.

North Portal To Gan

The village started expanding to the south in the late fourteenth century. In the fifteenth century, vineyards producing grapes for red and white wines were enlarged. The red wines brought a greater market value than the whites.

In the sixteenth century, a fire destroyed the whole village including the church, fabricator of cookware and common house. Three noble houses rebuilt in the sixteenth century show the same architectural feature: that of a spiral staircase housed in a tower next to the main building. The title of "City" was awarded to Gan by letters patent of Henry IV. Louis XIII confirmed this title in perpetuity when he declared that "the city of Gan enjoy now and forever the same honors and privileges as other cities Béarn." In 1633, a new canal was dug to supply water to a gristmill built in the same year. A stone found at the bottom of the channel states that in July 1633, the dam was completed at the expense of King Louis XIII.

Around 1740, Gan began to capture the mineral waters in the area and used for many years "to cure intermittent fevers, obstructions of any kind and certain tumors, and relieve nephritic." For almost a century, the waters were not used. The municipality restored the fountain in 1994.

Monein

A remarkable seven-story stone tower of the Église de St-Girons stands out from everywhere in Monein. Its size makes it the largest Gothic church of Béarn. The main structure has the form of an overturned double-hull vessel and was fabricated from heart oak.

During the sixteenth century, the village was growing with more than 5,000 inhabitants, compared to Pau with 700 inhabitants. The old church of St-Pee, or St-Pierre, was Romanesque in style and too small. Monein decided to build a larger church.

The village was also a rich community because it paid more taxes than Orthez and Oloron-Ste-Marie together. Finally, the population was very involved in religious life because there were nine priests and sixteen religious brotherhoods.

The dimensions of the new church were made proportional to the wealth of the village. It measures more than 61 meters long, 16 meters wide and 31 meters high, making it larger than the two cathedrals of Béarn.

It took 50 years to build starting in 1464. For 70 years, people funded the work through a number of taxes and erected the edifice with their own hands.

The Queen of Navarre, Jeanne d'Albret (acknowledged spiritual and political leader of the French Huguenot movement and also mother of Henry IV, the first Bourbon king of France), transformed this Catholic church to a Protestant church by stripping it of its furniture and threatened to destroy it. The local population remained Catholic and resisted their Queen's plans for destruction. It was spared and returned to Catholicism by the Edict of Integration of Béarn issued by King Louis XIII of France.

The church was returned to its origins and still retains Baroque furniture including a large altarpiece and a seventeenth century Toulouse organ.

St-Girons church was restored in the late twentieth and early twenty-first centuries. It is now a tourist attraction highlighted with a sound and light show.

Older Monein residents boast about the sunny summer holiday smells they once enjoyed. That happened in the peach orchards, but not just any peach, the Roussane peach.

This variety was typical of the region, characterized by a beautiful yellow color, stained red and very juicy. It was famous in the late nineteenth century and at that time the queen of the village peach and grape fairs.

Église St-Girons

Production had gradually disappeared in the 1960s, even with orchards on the hillsides. The Roussane peach, like the vine that produces the Jurançon grape, develops its uniqueness and high quality taste from the stony soil and the Béarnaise sun.

A group of thirty local farmers and winemakers has been working for seven years to revive production of the Roussane.

Queues and Directions

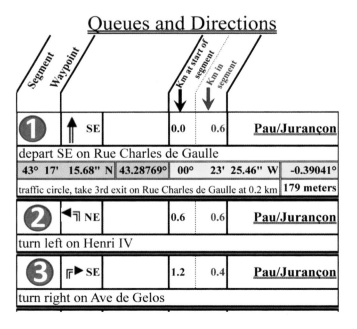

Segment	Waypoint		Km at start of segment	Km in segment	
①	↑ SE		0.0	0.6	**Pau/Jurançon**
depart SE on Rue Charles de Gaulle					
43° 17' 15.68" N	43.28769°	00° 23' 25.46" W			-0.39041°
traffic circle, take 3rd exit on Rue Charles de Gaulle at 0.2 km					179 meters
②	◄ NE		0.6	0.6	**Pau/Jurançon**
turn left on Henri IV					
③	► SE		1.2	0.4	**Pau/Jurançon**
turn right on Ave de Gelos					

(Waypoints continued on page 82)

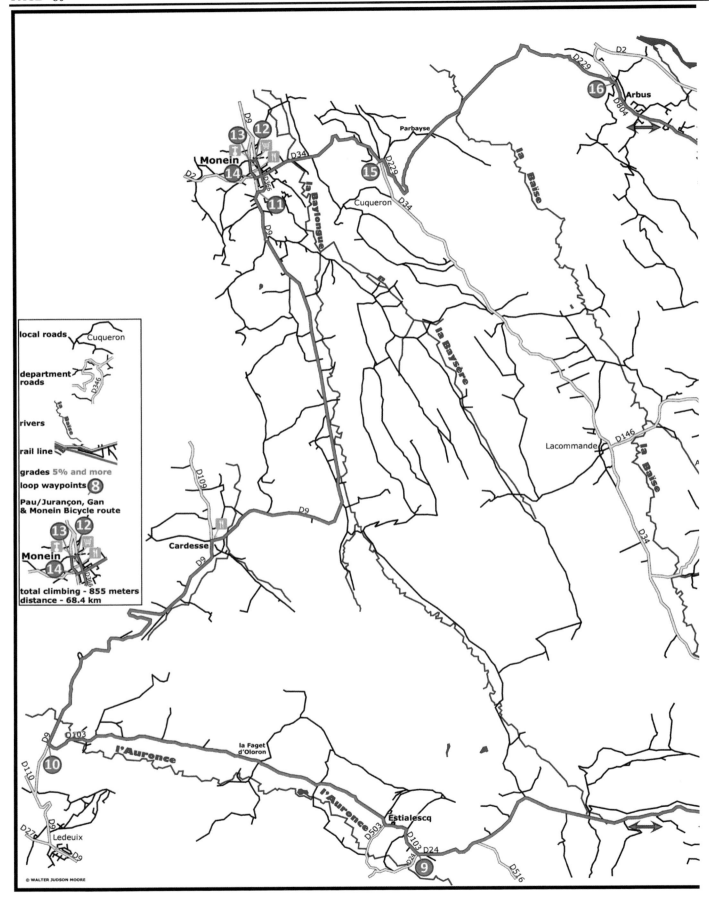

local roads

department
roads

rivers

rail line

grades 5% and more

loop waypoints (8)

Pau/Jurançon, Gan
& Monein Bicycle route

total climbing - 855 meters
distance - 68.4 km

© WALTER JUDSON MOORE

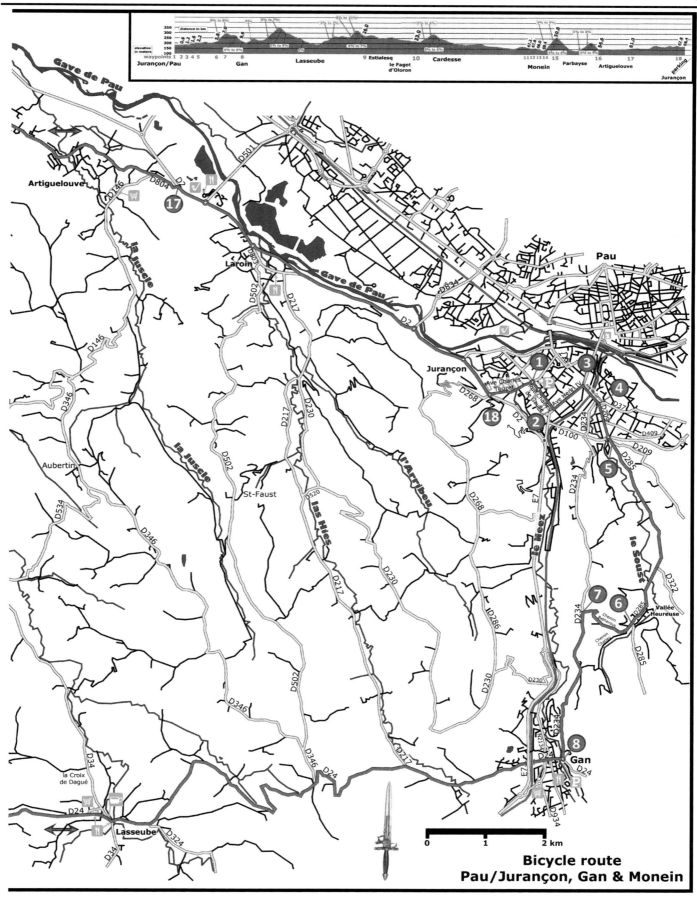

**Bicycle route
Pau/Jurançon, Gan & Monein**

(4) ⇨SE | **D209** | 1.6 | 0.6 | **Pau/Jurançon**

D234 on right, turn right on D209

(5) ◀⊙SE | **D285** | 2.2 | 3.6 | **Pau/Jurançon**

traffic circle, take 3rd exit on D285, D100 at 2nd exit

| 43° 16' 45.00" N | 43.27917° | 00° 22' 31.22" W | -0.37534° |

D322 on left at 4.8 km | **189 meters**

(6) ⇨SW | | 5.8 | 1.2 |

turn right on Chemin Betherous

| 43° 15' 01.77" N | 43.25049° | 00° 22' 14.18" W | -0.37061° |

5% to 8% ascents | **209 meters**

(7) ◀⊓ S | **D234** | 7.0 | 2.6 |

turn left on D234

| 43° 15' 08.00" N | 43.25222° | 00° 22' 50.57" W | -0.38071° |

6% to 8% descents | **285 meters**

(8) ⊙▶W | **D24** | 9.6 | 16.4 | **Gan**

traffic circle, take 1st exit on D24

| 43° 13' 47.71" N | 43.22992° | 00° 23' 05.32" W | -0.38481° |

cross under rail line & E7 at 10.2 km | 145 meter climb in 4.6 km | **208 meters**

5% ascent | D217 on right at 12.4 km

5% to 7% ascents | D346 on right at 14.6 km

5% to 9% descents | D324 on left at 19.0 km

Lasseube at 19.4 km | D34 on left at 19.8 km

135 meter climb in 5.4 km | D34 on right at 20.0 km

5% to 7% ascents | D516 on left at 25.0 km

5% to 7% descents

(9) ⇨NW | **D103** | 26.0 | 7.0 |

turn right on D103

| 43° 12' 54.46" N | 43.21513° | 00° 32' 49.66" W | -0.54713° |

Estialesq at 26.6 km | le Faget d'Oloron at 29.4 km | **270 meters**

(10) ⇨ N | **D9** | 33.0 | 14.2 |

turn right on D9

| 43° 13' 57.05" N | 43.23251° | 00° 37' 18.81" W | -0.62189° |

Cardesse, D109 straight ahead at 38.8 km | **222 meters**

5% to 6% ascents then 5% to 6% descents

traffic circle, 2nd exit on D9 at 46.2 km

(11) ⇨ E | **D366** | 47.2 | 0.6 | **Monein**

turn right on D366

| 43° 19' 03.10" N | 43.31753° | 00° 34' 41.66" W | -0.57824° |

| | | | **157 meters**

(12) ◀⊓ SW | | 47.8 | 0.2 | **Monein**

turn left toward Église St-Girons

(13) ◀⊓ SW | **D9** | 48.0 | 0.4 | **Monein**

turn left on D9

(14) ◀⊓ E | **D34** | 48.4 | 2.4 | **Monein**

turn left on D34

125 meter climb in 1.8 km | 5% to 9% ascents

(15) ◀⊓ NE | **D229** | 50.8 | 5.8 |

turn left on D229

| 43° 19' 18.84" N | 43.32190° | 00° 33' 11.25" W | -0.55313° |

5% to 8% descents | **Parabayse** at 52.8 km | **262 meters**

5% to 6% ascents, then 5% to 8% descents

(16) ⇨ SE | **D804** | 56.6 | 4.4 | **Arbus**

turn right on D804

| 43° 20' 02.81" N | 43.33411° | 00° 30' 24.47" W | -0.50680° |

Artiguelouve at 58.8 km | D146 on right at 60.6 km | **141 meters**

(17) ⇨ SE | **D2** | 61.0 | 6.6 |

turn right on D2

| 43° 19' 03.83" N | 43.31773° | 00° 27' 46.09" W | -0.46280° |

traffic circle, 1st exit on D2, D501 on 2nd exit at 61.6 km | **156 meters**

traffic circle, 3rd exit on D2, D803 on 2nd exit at 62.8 km

D803 on right at 63.6 km

traffic circle, 2nd exit on D2, D834 on 3rd exit at 65.8 km

traffic circle, 1st exit on D2 at 66.8 km

(18) ◀⊙ E | | 67.6 | 0.8 | **Pau/Jurançon**

traffic circle, take 3rd exit on Ave Charles Touzet

| 43° 17' 08.53" N | 43.28570° | 00° 23' 58.27" W | -0.39952° |

| | | | **179 meters**

| | | 68.4 | parking, **Pau/Jurançon**

Lasseube

18 Oloron-Ste-Marie & Col de Marie Blanque

Details:

Distance—61.8 kilometers

Climbing—1,000 meters

Challenge rank—8.5

Parking: Oloron-Ste-Marie at the southeast corner of Place Gambetta.

Bicycle northeast and east from Oloron-Ste-Marie to Précilhon then southeast to Arudy. From Arudy, cycle south to Bielle. Next, climb west and up to Col de Marie Blanque and coast down to Escot. Finally, follow the route north to Oloron.

There are two significant climbs on the route. The first starts in Oloron and climbs gradually, after an initial 8% jump, 200 meters in 16.6 kilometers. The second, often ranked as a first category climb in the 14 times used in the Tour de France, starts at Arudy and climbs 640 meters in 19.0 kilometers with 6% to 11% ascents. The descent down to Escot has grades up to 15%.

Oloron-Ste-Marie

In the first century of the Common Era (CE), Romans settled here and named it Iluro after an Aquitaine population related to the Iberians. Early Christians started a church dedicated to Ste-Marie on the alluvial terrace, which became the future cathedral and a citadel on the hill of Ste-Croix d'Oloron. The promontory of Ste-Croix was the oppidum. In 506 CE, the first bishop Gratus attended the Council of Agde with 34 Visigoth bishops. He became St-Gratus.

Town Center

The Vandal invasions plunged Iluro into oblivion. By 1058, some people had remained as Bishop Stephen of

Lavedan settled on the alluvial terrace. In 1080, Viscount Centulle of Béarn developed the new town of Oloron on the ancient Roman oppidum.

In the medieval times this promontory, bordered on the east and west by rivers, was very secure. Viscount Centulle encouraged people to live and trade in Oloron. He established legal and economic privileges with an act of *poblacion* (settlement) that was strengthened in 1220. The town became an important and welcoming stop for pilgrims on the road to St-Jacques-de-Compostela.

Meanwhile, the former Iluro city rose from the ashes with the name of its cathedral, Ste-Marie.

The descendants of the Viscount erected monuments upon their return from the Crusades. In 1214, Gaston VI was forced to cede Ste-Marie and the surrounding villages to the bishops as Albigensian heretics lived there.

In 1385, Oloron had 366 homes, Legugnon had 11 and Ste-Marie had 85.

At The Gave d'Ossau Bridge

The two communities — Oloron and Ste-Marie - became rivals for about eight centuries. In spite of the rivalry, Ste-Marie remained economically dependent on Oloron. In the thirteenth century, taking advantage of the Albigensian Crusade, the bishop obtained the lordship of Ste-Marie. In the fourteenth and the fifteenth centuries, Oloron gained the right to hold markets and fairs, which led to the creation of suburbs. The community was almost the economic capital of Béarn through its trade with Spain and the development of textile crafts.

The Wars of Religion and The Revolution twice suspended that prosperity. Arrival of the railway in 1883 and trade advances rebuilt the local economy.

The rich medieval past remains on view with timbered houses that had some of the stores.

Col de Marie Blanque

Col de Marie Blanque and Pic de Lourene

Starting from Louvie-Juzon and through the Vallée d'Ossau, the climb from the east is 15 kilometers long. Over this distance it gains 615 meters at an average of 4% ascent.

Bielle War Memorial

The climb proper starts at Bielle where it is 11.5 kilometers long, gaining 585 meters at an average 5% ascent, with a maximum of 11% near the start.

The western side of the climb starts from Escot. The climb is 9.3 kilometers long at an average of 7.8% ascent for an elevation gain of 715 meters. Although relatively short, there are several sections with gradients in excess of 15%.

The pass was first used in the Tour de France in 1978 and has been crossed 14 times by the tour, including on stage 17 of the 2010 tour from Pau to the Col du Tourmalet.

Église de l' Assomption-de-la-Bienheureuse-Vierge-Marie

Be aware that there may be cows in the road. Do slow down, they outweigh you and won't get out of the way. They are a breed of beef cattle known as Blondes d'Aquitaine, and have been bred here since the sixth century.

Gave d'Aspe Valley

This valley is one of three Pyrenean valleys bordering with Spain. Located south of Oloron-Ste-Marie, it is between the valleys of Ossau and Barétous.

Probably the harsher of the valleys, it spreads along the Aspe Rivière south until the famous 8.6 kilometer Aragon tunnel into Spain.

Major landscape attractions include the spires of the Cirque de Lescun and the entrance to the Col de Marie Blanque.

In summer, the Aspe valley is a mecca of hiking paths carved into the rocks.

Source of Pyrénées Chevre Fromage

The Pyrénées National Park goes through the valley.

Queues and Directions

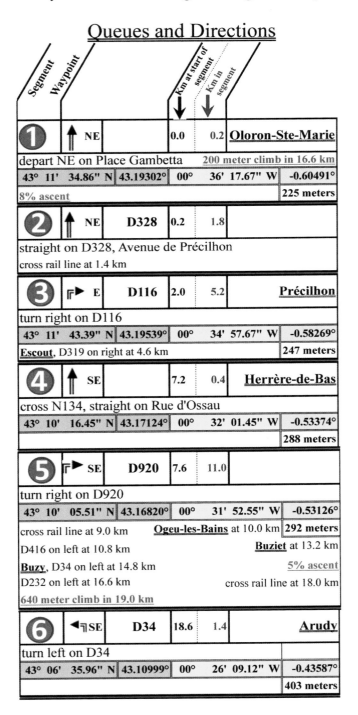

Segment	Waypoint		Km at start of segment	Km in segment	
1	↑ NE		0.0	0.2	**Oloron-Ste-Marie**
depart NE on Place Gambetta			200 meter climb in 16.6 km		
43° 11' 34.86" N	43.19302°	00°	36' 17.67" W		-0.60491°
8% ascent					225 meters
2	↑ NE	D328	0.2	1.8	
straight on D328, Avenue de Précilhon					
cross rail line at 1.4 km					
3	⌐▶ E	D116	2.0	5.2	**Précilhon**
turn right on D116					
43° 11' 43.39" N	43.19539°	00°	34' 57.67" W		-0.58269°
Escout, D319 on right at 4.6 km					247 meters
4	↑ SE		7.2	0.4	**Herrère-de-Bas**
cross N134, straight on Rue d'Ossau					
43° 10' 16.45" N	43.17124°	00°	32' 01.45" W		-0.53374°
					288 meters
5	⌐▶ SE	D920	7.6	11.0	
turn right on D920					
43° 10' 05.51" N	43.16820°	00°	31' 52.55" W		-0.53126°
cross rail line at 9.0 km	Ogeu-les-Bains at 10.0 km				292 meters
D416 on left at 10.8 km				Buziet at 13.2 km	
Buzy, D34 on left at 14.8 km				5% ascent	
D232 on left at 16.6 km			cross rail line at 18.0 km		
640 meter climb in 19.0 km					
6	◀⌐ SE	D34	18.6	1.4	**Arudy**
turn left on D34					
43° 06' 35.96" N	43.10999°	00°	26' 09.12" W		-0.43587°
					403 meters
7	◀⌐ E	D287	20.0	0.8	**Arudy**
turn left on D287					
43° 06' 13.23" N	43.10368°	00°	25' 33.61" W		-0.42600°
					408 meters
8	⌐▶ SE	D934	20.8	5.2	
turn right on D934					
43° 06' 11.18" N	43.10311°	00°	24' 55.47" W		-0.41541°
D3920 on right then traffic circle, 2nd exit on D934 at 23.0 km					409 meters
9	⊙ SW	D294	26.0	0.4	
traffic circle, take 2nd exit on D294					
43° 03' 36.49" N	43.06014°	00°	25' 37.53" W		-0.42709°
					440 meters
10	↑ SW	D3934	26.4	0.2	
straight on D3934					
11	⌐▶ W		26.6	1.0	**Bielle**
turn right through Bielle			7% to 11% ascents		
43° 03' 19.70" N	43.05547°	00°	25' 52.63" W		-0.43129°
					455 meters
12	◀⌐ W	D294	27.6	19.4	
turn left on D294			6% to 11% ascents		
43° 03' 26.90" N	43.05747°	00°	26' 20.12" W		-0.43892°
Col de Marie Blanque at 37.8 km 5% to 15% decents					503 meters
13	⌐▶ N	D238	47.0	12.6	**Escot**
turn right on D238					
43° 04' 36.09" N	43.07669°	00°	36' 22.10" W		-0.60614°
cross D918 at 51.8 km		D638 on right at 54.4 km			338 meters
Oloron-Sœix at 58.2 km			D338 on right at 59.4 km		
14	⌐▶ N	D328	59.6	2.0	
turn right on D328					
43° 10' 42.50" N	43.17847°	00°	36' 08.03" W		-0.60223°
					234 meters
15	⌐▶ NE		61.6	0.2	**Oloron-Ste-Marie**
turn right on Rue Justice, cross Gave d'Ossau					
43° 11' 32.50" N	43.19236°	00°	36' 25.43" W		-0.60706°
					222 meters
			61.8	parking, **Oloron-Ste-Marie**	

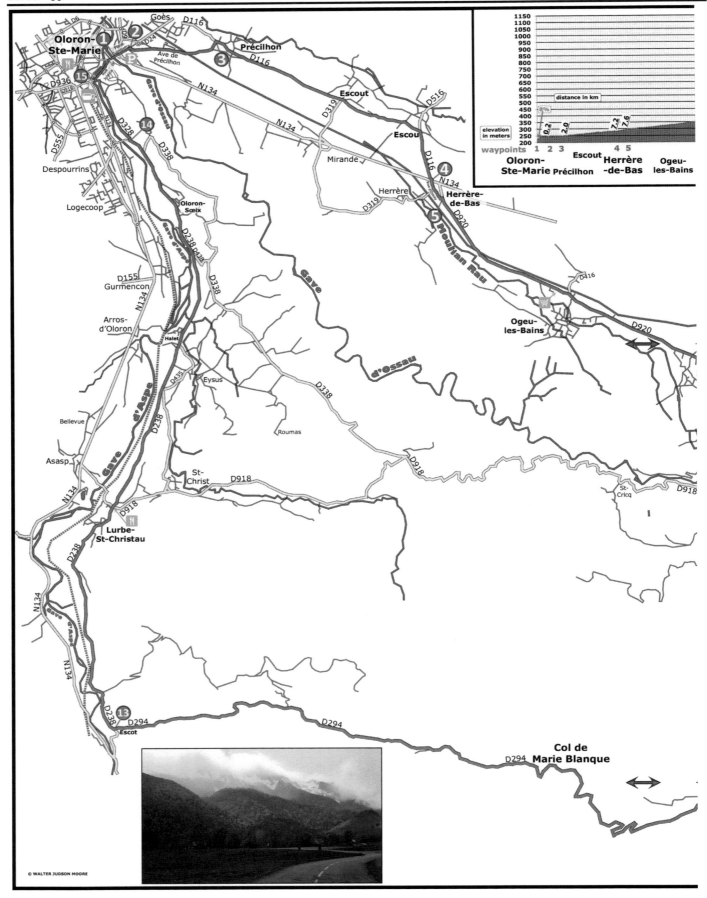

Oloron-Ste-Marie

Goès

Précilhon

Escout

Escou

Mirande

Herrère

Herrère-de-Bas

Moullian Rau

Ogeu-les-Bains

Despourrins

Logecoop

Oloron-Scex

Gurmencon

Arros-d'Oloron

Halet

Eysus

Bellevue

Roumas

Asasp

St-Christ

Lurbe-St-Christau

St-Crlcq

Escot

Col de Marie Blanque

elevation in meters
distance in km
waypoints

Oloron-Ste-Marie   Précilhon   Escout   Herrère-de-Bas   Ogeu-les-Bains

© WALTER JUDSON MOORE

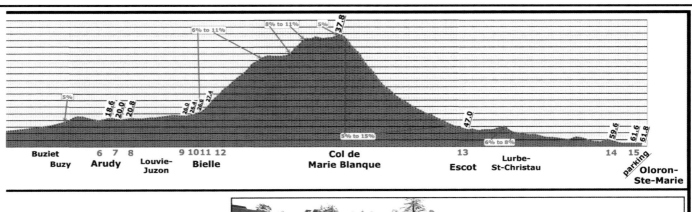

Buziet — Buzy — Arudy — Louvie-Juzon — Bielle — Col de Marie Blanque — Escot — Lurbe-St-Christau — Oloron-Ste-Marie

Col de MARIE BLANQUE (1035 m)

local roads
department roads
rivers
rail line
abondoned rail line
grades 5% and more
loop waypoints 8
Oloron-Ste-Marie & Col de Marie Blanque Bicycle route

total climbing - 1,000 meters
distance - 61.8 km

0   1   2 km

**Bicyle route
Oloron-Ste-Marie &
Col de Marie Blanque**

19 Col d'Aubisque

Details:

Distance—84.8 kilometers

Climbing—1,710 meters

Challenge rank—15.6

Parking: next to the church in Asson.

From Asson, bicycle and climb south 29 kilometers to the Col de Soulor. After Col de Soulor, cycle west 22½ kilometers over Col d'Aubisque to Eaux-Bonnes. Then follow the route north 15¼ kilometers through the stunning Ossau Valley to Louvie-Juzon. Finally, ride east and southeast 18¼ kilometers to Asson.

Asson

The route has two strenuous climbs. The first starts shortly after departing Asson and climbs 1,125 meters in 26 kilometers with 5% to 14% ascents, with the steepest grades approaching Col de Soulor. The second climb starts at the bottom of the 3.0-kilometer descent from Col de Soulor and climbs 400 meters in 6.4 kilometers with 5% to 13% ascents.

Arbéost

A Flock and The Goatherd

The village was established as a parish in 1743.

The population at the time was primarily involved in agricultural activities. The goatherds of Arbéost were known for the quality of the milk from their goats. From the nineteenth century, and until 1930, some went on the road at the end of the summer with their herd to sell milk in cities such as Bordeaux, and sometimes Paris. In the years from 1930 to 1962, a large number of the village men worked as miners in

the Baburet mine. Many of the young people worked for the summer season in the Lourdes hotels.

Col d'Aubisque

The pass is on the northern slopes of the Pic de Ger (2,613 meters) and connects the Ossau Valley to the Gave de Pau valley, via the Col du Soulor. It is generally closed from December to June.

Col du Soulor in The Rain

The east side ascends after the Col du Soulor (1,474 m). From the Soulor, the climb is 10.6 kilometers. The road from the Soulor runs along cliffs in the Cirque du Litor, where there are two short, narrow tunnels. From the Cirque du Litor, the climb is 7.5 kilometers at an average ascent of 5%.

The Col d'Aubisque appeared in the Tour de France in 1910. It has appeared frequently since then, about every other year. It was first included at the insistence of Alphonse Steinès, a colleague of Henri Desgrange of the Tour de France. Steinès visited the man responsible for local roads who told him "Take the riders up the Aubisque? You're completely crazy in Paris." Steinès agreed that the Tour would pay 5,000 francs to clear the pass. Desgrange knocked the price down to 2,000.

In 1951, Wim van Est was in the yellow jersey – the first Dutchman to wear it and chasing the leaders towards the Soulor when he slipped on gravel and fell into a ravine. He said:

"That first bend was wet, slippery from the snow. And there were sharp stones on the road that the cars had kicked up, and my front wheel hit them and I went over. Well, there was a drop of 70 meters. They've built a barrier there now but then there was nothing to stop you going over. I fell 70 meters, rolling and rolling and rolling. My feet had come out of the straps, my bike had disappeared, and there was a little flat area, the only one that's there, no bigger than the seat of a chair, and I landed on my backside. A meter left or right and I'd have dropped on to solid stone, six or seven hundred meters down. My ankles were all hurt, my elbows were *kaput*. I was all bruised and shaken up and I didn't know where I was, but nothing was broken."

The team's manager took a towrope from the Dutch team's car. It was too short to reach van Est and so he tied 40 racing tires to the rope. That was how he was pulled out. Van Est said: "It was all the tires that they had for the team. By the time they'd tugged me up, they were all stretched and they wouldn't stay on the wheels any more! Forty tires! I wanted to get back on my bike and start racing again. But I couldn't. The manager stopped the whole team."

Van Est told journalists: "I had the feeling that I was taking that bend badly but I so much wanted to keep the yellow jersey, so I went flat out and off I flew."

Vallée d'Ossau

The valley stretches from north to south about fifty kilometers from Rébénacq (fifteen kilometers from Pau) to the Spanish border. The lower part is the valley around Arudy are the foothills of the Pyrénées. The high valley includes low, average and high mountains. It is crossed by the Gave d'Ossau and dominated by the Pic du Midi d'Ossau at 2,884 meters.

Gave d'Ossau at Louvie-Juzon

It is the easternmost of the three main valleys carving the Béarn Pyrénées.

Louvie-Juzon

The Vallée d'Ossau connects with the Vallée d'Ouzom to the east by the Col d'Aubisque.

In the villages of the valley, homes and farm buildings are clustered around narrow streets that cling to the slopes. Gardens, orchards and pastures prosper when you move away from the homes. This organization clarifies the integration of the villages in the countryside.

Blondes d'Aquitaine

Queues and Directions

Segment	Waypoint			Km at start of segment	Km in segment	
①	↑	S	D126	0.0	12.4	**Asson**
depart S on D126						
43° 08' 28.39" N	43.14122°	00°	15' 20.52" W			-0.25570°
cross D35 at 0.2 km			D626 on left at 0.6 km			**322 meters**
D226 on left at 2.8 km			**1,145 meter ascent in 26.0 km**			
5% to 7% ascents			**Arthez-d'Asson** at 6.4 km			
D326 on left at 9.4 km						
②	⇨	S	D426	12.4	1.0	
turn right on D426						
43° 02' 36.74" N	43.04354°	00°	15' 49.64" W			-0.26379°
5% ascent						**466 meters**
③	↑	SE	D126	13.4	15.4	
straight on D126					**5% to 14% ascents**	
Arbéost at 20.2 km						

(Waypoints continued on page 92)

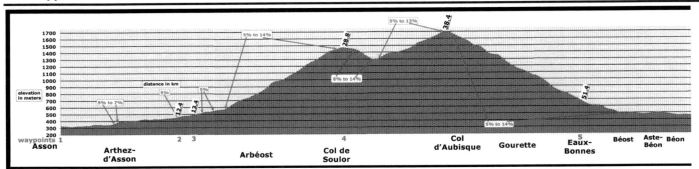

elevation in meters

distance in km

5% to 7%   5%   5%   5% to 14%   5% to 13%   38.4

6% to 14%   28.8

5% to 14%   51.4

12.4   13.4

waypoints 1
Asson

2   3

**Arthez-
d'Asson**

Arbéost

4

**Col de
Soulor**

**Col
d'Aubisque**

Gourette

5
**Eaux-
Bonnes**

Béost

**Aste-
Béon**

Béon

Bielle

Laruns

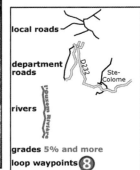

local roads

**department
roads**

D232

Ste-
Colome

rivers

grades 5% and more

loop waypoints (8)

**Col d'Aubisque
Bicycle route**

Louvie-
Juzon

D920   D35

(6)

**total climbing - 1,710 meters
distance - 84.8 km**

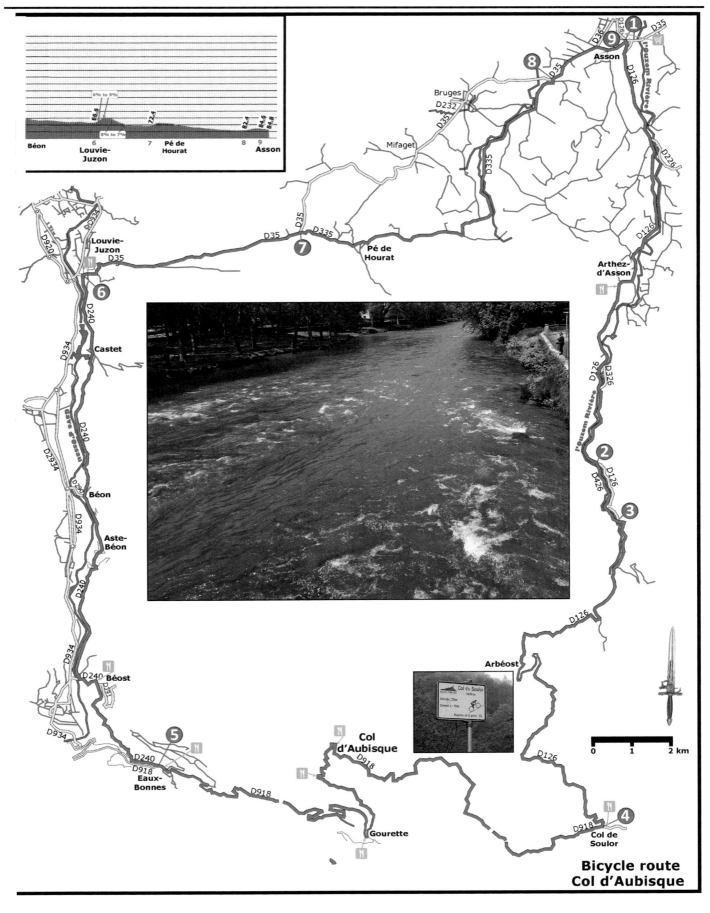

6% to 9%

66.6

5% to 7%

72.4

82.4 84.6 84.8

Béon

6

Louvie-
Juzon

7

Pé de
Hourat

8

9

Asson

D934

D920

Louvie-
Juzon

D35

6

D240

D934

Castet

D240

Gave d'Ossau

D2934

D290

Béon

D934

Aste-
Béon

D240

D934

D240

Béost

D240

D934

5

D240

D918

Eaux-
Bonnes

D918

Gourette

Col
d'Aubisque

D918

Col
d'Aubisque

Bruges

D232

D35

Mifaget

D335

D35

D35

D35

D335

7

Pé de
Hourat

Arthez-
d'Asson

D126

D326

Pouzom Rivière

2

D426

D126

3

D126

Arbéost

D126

D918

D126

4

D918

Col de
Soulor

8

D35

Asson

9

D36

1

D126

D35

Pouzom Rivière

D126

D226

D126

0   1   2 km

**Bicycle route
Col d'Aubisque**

④	⟥► W	D918	28.8	22.6	**Col de Soulor**
turn right on D918					
42° 57' 38.44" N	42.96068°	00°	15' 42.74" W		-0.26187°
6% to 14% descents	400 meter ascent in 6.4 km				1,471 meters
5% to 13% ascents	**Col d'Aubisque** at 38.4 km				
5% to 14% descents	**Gourette** at 42.8 km				
Eaux-Bonnes at 50.8 km					

⑤	⟥►NW	D240	51.4	15.2	**Eaux-Bonnes**
bear right on D240					
42° 58' 26.98" N	42.97416°	00°	23' 41.98" W		-0.39499°
Béost, D240e straight ahead at 55.2 km					662 meters
Aste-Béon at 59.0 km	**Béon**, D290 on left at 60.6 km				
Castet at 64.6 km					

⑥	⟥► E	D35	66.6	5.8	**Louvie-Juzon**
turn right on D35					
43° 05' 10.75" N	43.08632°	00°	25' 10.63" W		-0.41962°
6% to 9% ascents followed by 5% to 7% descents					420 meters

⑦	⟥► E	D335	72.4	10.0	
turn right on D335					
43° 05' 48.08" N	43.09669°	00°	21' 11.77" W		-0.35327°
Pé de Hourat at 74.2 km					369 meters

⑧	⟥►NE	D35	82.4	2.2	
turn right on D35					
43° 07' 53.72" N	43.13159°	00°	16' 36.32" W		-0.27676°
D36 on left at 83.8 km					307 meters

⑨	◄⟤ N	D126	84.6	0.2	**Asson**
turn left on D126					
43° 08' 25.24" N	43.14034°	00°	15' 17.78" W		-0.25494°
					322 meters

			84.8		parking, **Asson**

Road From Louvie-Juzon

Approaching Col de Soulor

20 Gan, Nay & Arudy

Details:

Distance—67.7 kilometers

Climbing—975 meters

Challenge rank—7.3

Parking: Place de la Mairie in Gan.

From Place de la Mairie cycle east 10 kilometers to Pardies-Piétat. After Pardies-Piétat, bicycle south and then west 26½ kilometers through Nay, Asson and Bruges to Louvie-Juzon. Then follow the route north and east 31 kilometers through Arudy and Lasseube back to Gan.

The route has four climbs. The first starts in Gan and climbs 105 meters in 2.6 kilometers with 5% to 8% ascents. The second climb starts as the route crosses D322 and climbs 140 meters in 2.6 kilometers with 5% to 7% ascents. The third, and longest ascent starts in Pardies-Piétat, climbing 275 meters in 25.4 kilometers with 5% to 8% ascents. The last hill starts in Lasseube rising 165 meters in 6.0 kilometers with 5% to 7% ascents.

Gan

Porte de Nord

Gaston II de Foix-Béarn established the community in 1335.

In 1385, Gan had 175 houses with approximately 900 residents. Local records of the fifteenth century report the existence of vineyards raising grapes for red wine and white wine. Vineyard and wine making activities lasted until the early nineteenth century.

In the sixteenth century, a fire destroyed most of the village. Three large, sixteenth century houses are still visible with similar architectural features such as a spiral staircase housed in a tower or two buildings connected by an angled tower with a staircase.

In 1633, a new canal was dug to supply a gristmill built in the same year. This mill was transformed in 1839 into a marble cutting and finishing workshop.

Around 1740, Gan began to exploit the known mineral waters in the area that were used for many years "to cure intermittent fevers, obstructions of any kind and certain tumors, and relieve nephritic." These thermal waters were the subject of a publication by the royal physician. For almost a century, the waters were no longer used. Gan restored the fountain in 1994.

The Mairie is typical of the nineteenth century, with halls on the ground floor. Some arches of the oldest hall are still visible in the current building.

Nay

The Viscountess of Béarn founded this bastide in 1302 after she purchased the land from the Hôpital Ste-Christine de Gabas. A fire of unknown origin destroyed Nay in 1534. The Wars of Religion followed, and in 1569, Catholics ransacked the town. Huguenots returned with a vengeance. Nay became an industrial city specializing in the manufacture of textiles, which thrived in the area.

Its geographical location explained how the town developed. It is located at the foot of the hills, had a ford across the Gave (river) de Pau, there is a path between Pau and Lourdes, and it controls access to the valley that connects to the Ossau valley by Arudy.

The workshops associated with textile making were organized by specialties and were diverse. For example, there were carders, shearers, spinners and embroiderers.

The manufacturer Royale Drapery & Dyeing in Nay was established probably around 1558. Royal Drapery was responsible for producing pieces of cloth, and included a weaving workshop that brought together under one roof several trades. All functioned only a short time before the Wars of Religion. It took two centuries for the industry to revive.

Place de la République

During the eighteenth century, there was a large increase in workshops throughout the Nay and Pau area. These workshops were all within eight kilometers of Nay. Factories near the river specialized in fabricated woolen blankets and Kadis (large homespun cloth).

In the city center, the Poey d'Oloron brothers manufactured Turkish Royale Beanies around 1740. These wool caps were exported to the eastern Mediterranean.

The revival of the textile industry in the nineteenth century differs from the sixteenth century by a major characteristic. Industrial engineering revived production mainly by the contribution of new technical specialties and mechanical innovations.

D636 Bridge Over Gave de Pau

The wool workshops manufactured woolen cloth, blankets and the knitted beret. Now, there are the only two remaining factories for berets in France. And there is a museum here for the beret.

A flood in 1826 destined the bridge of the time for replacement. The temporary bridge, built in 1834, was very expensive for the municipality. A new permanent bridge was planned for in 1828. This new bridge was in line with the market place and required the demolition of houses next to the square. It was completed in 1869.

Arudy

Development of the village started in the twelfth and thirteenth centuries as a Basque community.

A nineteenth century map shows that the structure of the city has changed little since the Middle Ages.

Église St-Germain in Place de l'Hôtel de Ville

The fifteenth and sixteenth century church, dedicated to St-Germain, has a polygonal apse, an altarpiece and paintings from the seventeenth and eighteenth centuries, along with gilded wood statues of St-Michael, St-Anastase and St-Lawrence.

The Mairie was built in the second half of the nineteenth century, with plans dated 1867. After some ups and downs, the construction was restarted in June 1871 and was finished in December 1873. It is a large stone building in the heart of the village, opposite the parish church, it has markets on the ground floor and open arcades on the perimeter.

Calhau-de-Teberne Dolmen Near Buzy

Lasseube

Baron Lescun recognized Lasseube in 1376, under the right of Gaston III Phoebus, who said, "Our charming village has developed on the banks of the river astride majestic stone bridges." It runs through the lush and fertile hills winding through the Jurançon vineyards.

Église Ste-Catherine

In the forest around the area lived bands of robbers before the village was known. Today the forest covers a substantial part of the territory, with nearly 1,700 hectares for fans of mushrooms or fresh air.

The rare Camarelet Lasseube variety of vines was named after the village.

Église Ste-Catherine was built in the late sixteenth century. Situated in the village center, it has an imposing steep roof. The remarkable south side has a striking Gothic portal. Two Gothic arches attract attention, including that of the sacristy door.

Rue Louis Barthou

Typical Béarnaise houses surround the church.

Queues and Directions

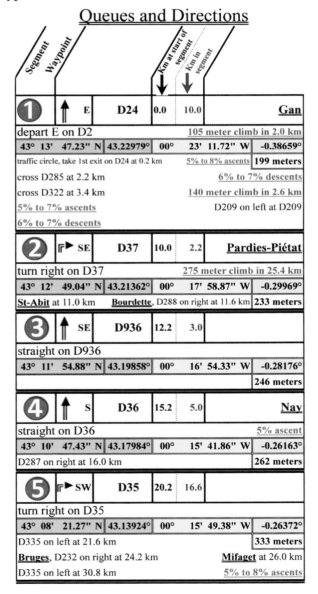

Segment	Waypoint			Km at start of segment	Km in segment	
1	↑	E	D24	0.0	10.0	**Gan**
depart E on D2					105 meter climb in 2.0 km	
43° 13' 47.23" N	43.22979°	00°	23' 11.72" W	-0.38659°		
traffic circle, take 1st exit on D24 at 0.2 km				5% to 8% ascents		199 meters
cross D285 at 2.2 km				6% to 7% descents		
cross D322 at 3.4 km				140 meter climb in 2.6 km		
5% to 7% ascents				D209 on left at D209		
6% to 7% descents						
2	⇒	SE	D37	10.0	2.2	**Pardies-Piétat**
turn right on D37				275 meter climb in 25.4 km		
43° 12' 49.04" N	43.21362°	00°	17' 58.87" W	-0.29969°		
St-Abit at 11.0 km		Bourdette, D288 on right at 11.6 km				233 meters
3	↑	SE	D936	12.2	3.0	
straight on D936						
43° 11' 54.88" N	43.19858°	00°	16' 54.33" W	-0.28176°		
						246 meters
4	↑	S	D36	15.2	5.0	**Nay**
straight on D36				5% ascent		
43° 10' 47.43" N	43.17984°	00°	15' 41.86" W	-0.26163°		
D287 on right at 16.0 km						262 meters
5	⇒	SW	D35	20.2	16.6	
turn right on D35						
43° 08' 21.27" N	43.13924°	00°	15' 49.38" W	-0.26372°		
D335 on left at 21.6 km						333 meters
Bruges, D232 on right at 24.2 km				Mifaget at 26.0 km		
D335 on left at 30.8 km				5% to 8% ascents		
6	⇒	N	D3920	36.8	2.0	**Louvie-Juzon**
turn right on D3920, D240 on left						
43° 05' 09.23" N	43.08590°	00°	25' 19.76" W	-0.42216°		
						417 meters
7	⊙⇒	E	D53	38.8	0.6	**Arudy**
traffic circle, take 1st exit on D53						
43° 06' 03.29" N	43.10091°	00°	26' 00.64" W	-0.43351°		
						418 meters
8	⇐	N		39.4	0.4	**Arudy**
turn left on Place du Foirail						
9	↑	N		39.8	0.6	**Arudy**
continue toward D920						
10	⇒	N	D920	40.4	4.0	
turn right on D920						
43° 06' 36.02" N	43.11001°	00°	26' 09.22" W	-0.43589°		
						405 meters
11	⇒	NE	D34	44.4	3.4	**Buzy**
turn right on D34						
43° 08' 06.53" N	43.13515°	00°	27' 34.73" W	-0.45965°		
cross old rail line at 45.2 km		cross under rail line at 46.8 km				366 meters
12	⇒	E	N134	47.8	0.6	
turn right on N134				6% ascent		
43° 09' 42.62" N	43.16184°	00°	27' 28.26" W	-0.45785°		
						401 meters
13	⇐	NW	D34	48.4	8.6	**Belair**
turn left across highway onto D34						
43° 09' 45.44" N	43.16262°	00°	27' 03.67" W	-0.45102°		
5% to 10% descents						433 meters
14	⇐	NW	D24	57.0	0.4	**Lasseube**
turn left on D24						
43° 13' 13.95" N	43.22054°	00°	28' 35.56" W	-0.47654°		
						181 meters
15	↶	SE	D24	57.4	10.3	**Lasseube**
U-turn on D24				165 meter climb in 6.0 km		
D324 on right at 58.4 km				5% to 7% ascents		
D346 on left at 62.8 at km				D217 on left at 65.0 km		
cross under N134 & rail line at 67.2 km						
				67.7		parking, **Gan**

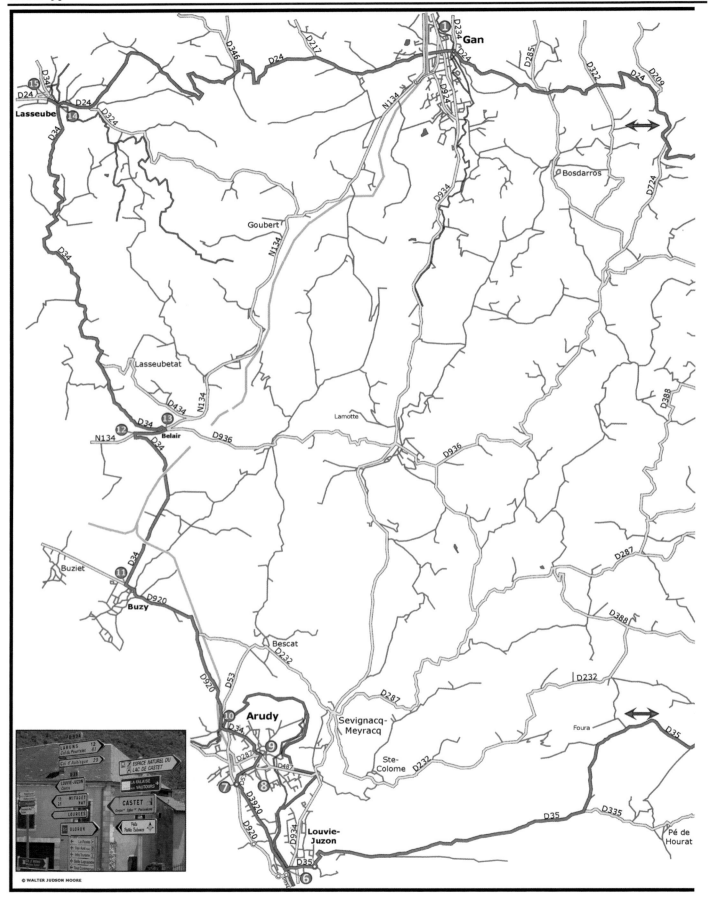

© WALTER JUDSON MOORE

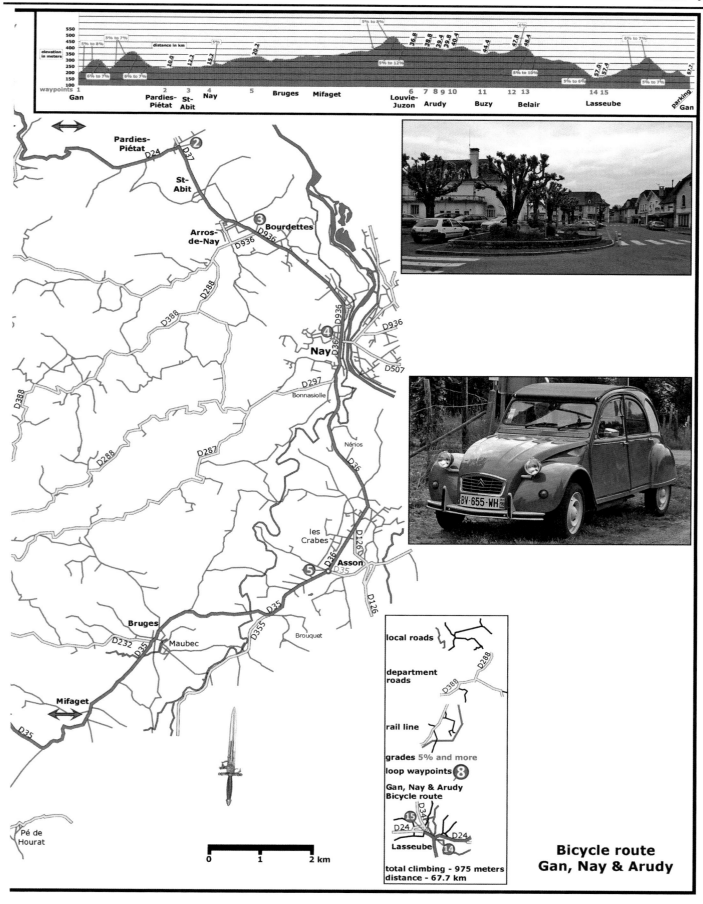

**Bicycle route
Gan, Nay & Arudy**

21 Col du Tourmalet, Col d'Aspin & Campan

There are two routes in this section: the Col du Tourmalet, and the Col d'Aspin. Should you decide to cycle both routes, climb the Tourmalet first, descend to Ste-Marie-de-Campan and turn right to climb the Col d'Aspin. The distance of the combined climbs is 71.7 kilometers, climbing is 2,150 meters and the challenge rank is 19.8. There are 60 ascents between 5% and 10%, and 35 ascents over 10%. The difficulty of a same day, combined route is beyond the scope of this guidebook.

Col du Tourmalet Details:

Distance—46.1 kilometers

Climbing—1,520 meters

Challenge rank—15.2

Parking: at the lot near D8 in Campan.

Bicycle southeast 6 kilometers through Campan to Ste-Marie-de-Campan. From the right turn in Ste-Marie-de-Campan (famous TV vantage point the real climb up this famous pass) climb 17 kilometers through la Mongie to the summit. From the summit, retrace the route back to Campan.

Take careful note of the sign in Ste-Marie-de-Campan listing avalanche warnings. D918 is the highest paved road in the Pyrénées.

There is one massive climb on the route. It starts at the parking lot in Campan and steeply climbs 1,479 meters in 23 kilometers with 5% to 16% ascents.

Campan and its Valley

Campan Valley Toward Col du Tourmalet From Ste-Marie-de-Campan

Settlement of people in the Campan valley left signs of Proto-Celtic civilization. The first historical people that came here were probably the Bigerri near Tarbes. Campan is reasonably the Roman settlement of Domain Campanus. During the Gallic Wars, Julius Caesar delegated his lieutenant Crassus the task of

conquering what today is southern France. Caesar visited the Campan valley during his eighth season.

A market located in Bagnères-de-Bigorre (located halfway between Lourdes and Campan) where trades took place between farmers of the eastern Adour plain and the mountain shepherds. Wool woven by local artisans provided the raw material for bigerri jackets, capes in warm, loose wool in white or brown, which were so successful that they were known in Rome.

Grip and the Campan Valley

Historically, shepherds of the Aure and Campan valleys fought for possession of the rich grasslands. It was common after the snows melted, to find the body of a shepherd at the bottom of a valley or stream, a victim of fights between the two parties. To end this fight that killed too many young men, an alderman from each of the valleys organized a duel. The border would be set where the defeated combatant died.

Marble Quarry at les Quatre Véziaux

Both camps got ready. On the Campan side, there was a huge and strong contender. He was so big and nasty that he was called the Great Dane.

The Aure side was discouraged by the bold stories about the Great Dane. Nobody volunteered and everyone was afraid. Finally Fréchou, a small and ugly shepherd, took up the challenge. His Aure neighbors believed in advance that he would be defeated.

When the day came, the two contenders met on a grassy ridge. The crowd was large, but the atmosphere was more relaxed among the Campan people. Seeing his opponent, the Great Dane shouted to his side: "gentlemen of Campan, the mountain is ours!" The fight began, and after a few passes, it did not proceed as anyone might have predicted. Fréchou sidestepped his enemy and let him fall on a rocky outcrop. The Great Dane broke his ribs and could not move, but he was not dead.

Then began an incredible scene. Fréchou bound the feet of his opponent and started to drag him down to Payolle (which is now on the road to Col d'Aspin). The Aure people encouraged Fréchou; the Campan people booed their champion. The Campan women threw stones and shouted, "Die now!" Then Aure women extended their aprons and told Fréchou "Easy small man, do not kill him too fast!"

The defeated contender was dragged to the meadow of St-Jean, upstream from Payolle, which today is the les Quatre Véziaux boundary.

Église St-Jean-Baptiste

The Campan church of St-Jean-Baptiste was constructed in the sixteenth century and contains a baroque altarpiece dating from the eighteenth century. The monument to the dead of Campan was sculpted and erected in 1926 at the front of the church and is distinguished by its sober appearance. Unlike the heroic soldiers who decorate many of the war memorials in France, the statue that dominates this monument represents a meditating woman, her face practically invisible, who wears the traditional clothing of the people of the valley.

In the old days, when a man of the Campan valley got married in circumstances that were not normal, for example when an old widower married a young girl, he was the object of a charivari (pandemonium), an outbreak of rough mockery. Representing the couple were coarse dolls, known as les Mounaques (from the Occitan word monaca, meaning doll or puppet).

For some years, a workshop has been open in Campan manufacturing a collection of small mounaques. It has been located since 1999 at the heart of Campan, in a house provided by the municipal council. In summer, displays of mounaques can sometimes be seen around the town.

The Forge of Ste-Marie-de-Campan is one of the high places of the Tour de France. The famous cyclist, Eugène Christophe, known as le Vieux Gaulois (the Old Gaul), repaired the front fork of his bicycle there after being struck by a car during the descent of the Tourmalet in the 1913 race. The rules of the race prevented him from obtaining assistance and he had to walk 15 kilometers and then do his own repair. This gave the leading pack an advance of four hours and Christophe's dreams of victory evaporated.

Col du Tourmalet

The Col du Tourmalet (2,115 meters / 6,939 feet) is the highest road in the Pyrénées. Ste-Marie-de-Campan is at the foot on the eastern side and the ski station La Mongie is two-thirds of the way up. Luz-St-Sauveur is at the bottom of the western side.

Starting from Ste-Marie-de-Campan, the climb is 17.2 kilometers, gaining 1,268 meters, at an average 7.4% ascent with a maximum of 16% near the top of the pass. As with most French climbs, each kilometer is marked by the distance to the summit and the average gradient of the next kilometer.

From the pass itself, a path leads to the Pic du Midi de Bigorre observatory (2,877 meters).

Pic du Midi de Bigorre (center)

The Col du Tourmalet is one of the more famous climbs on the Tour de France. It has been included more than any other pass, starting in 1910, when the Pyrénées were introduced. The first rider over was Octave Lapize, the winner in Paris.

The Ascent 730 Meters Below the Summit

As of the 2011 edition of the Tour de France, the Col du Tourmalet has been crossed 76 times in the Tour's history, plus a stage finish at the summit in 1974. There have also been three finishes at La Mongie. Since 1980 it has been ranked *hors catégorie*, (above categorizing). The Vuelta a España has crossed the pass several times.

One of Many Snow Sheds

At the pass there is a memorial to Jacques Goddet, director of the Tour de France from 1936 to 1987, and a large statue of Octave Lapize gasping for air as he struggles to make the climb.

The Pyrénées were included in the Tour de France at the insistence of Alphonse Steinès, a colleague of the organizer, Henri Desgrange. Steinès agreed to pay 5,000 francs, knocked down to 2,000 by Desgrange, to include the Col d'Aubisque and Tourmalet. Steinès came back to investigate the Tourmalet, starting at the inn opposite the church in Ste-Marie-de-Campan with sausage, ham and cheese. He hired a driver called Dupont, from Bagnères-de-Bigorre. Dupont and Steinès made it the first 16 kilometers, after which their car came to a stop. Dupont and Steinès started to walk but Dupont turned back after 600 meters, shouting "The bears come over from Spain when it snows." Steinès set off. He mistook voices in the

darkness for thieves. They were youngsters guarding sheep with their dog. Steinès called to one.

"Son, do you know the Tourmalet well? Could you guide me? I'll give you a gold coin. When we get to the other top, I'll give you another one."

The boy joined him but then turned back.

Steinès rested on a rock. He considered sitting it out until dawn, and then realized he would freeze. He slipped on the icy road, and then fell into a stream. He climbed back to the road and again fell in the snow. Exhausted and stumbling, he heard another voice. (This reads like my first day cycling in Bordeaux, but not anywhere close to Steinès' misery.)

"Tell me who goes there or I'll shoot."

"I'm a lost traveller. I've just come across the Tourmalet."

"Oh, it's you, Monsieur Steinès. We were expecting you. We got a phone call at Ste-Marie-de-Campan. Everybody's at Barèges. It's coming on three o'clock. There are search teams of guides out looking for you."

The organizing newspaper, *L'Auto*, had a correspondent at Barèges, a man called Lanne-Camy. He took Steinès for a bath and provided new clothes.

Steinès sent a telegram to Desgrange, "Crossed Tourmalet stop. Very good road stop. Perfectly feasible."

la Mongie

Shops, Restaurants and Hotels

Col du Tourmalet Waypoints

Queues and Directions

Segment	Waypoint			Km at start of segment	Km in segment	
①	↑ W	D8	0.0	0.2		**Campan**
depart W on D8						
43° 01' 03.93" N	43.01776°	00°	42' 10.48" E			0.70541°
1,479 meter ascent in 23.2 km						659 meters
②	◄⅂ SE	D935	0.2	6.0		**Campan**
turn left on D935					**St-Roch** at 1.8 km	
D154 on right at 4.2 km						5% to 9% ascents
③	⌐► S	D918	6.2	17.0		**Ste-Marie-de-Campan**
turn right on D918						5% to 16% ascents
42° 59' 04.68" N	42.98463°	00°	13' 39.00" E			0.22750°
Gripp at 10.8 km			1st snowshed at 17.0 km			861 meters
3 snowsheds at 17.8 km						**la Mongie** at 18.8 km
④	⌐↓ NE	D918	23.2	17.0		**Col du Tourmalet**
U-turn on D918						5% to 16% descents
42° 54' 29.57" N	42.90821°	00°	08' 42.28" E			0.14508°
la Mongie at 27.2 km			3 snowsheds at 27.2 km			2,138 meters
1st snowshed at 29.2 km						**Gripp** at 35.6 km
⑥	◄⅂ N	D935	40.2	5.8		**Ste-Marie-de-Campan**
turn left on D935						5% to 9% descents
42° 59' 04.68" N	42.98463°	00°	13' 39.00" E			0.22750°
D154 on left at 41.8 km			**St-Roch** at 44.2 km			861 meters
⑦	⌐► E	D8	46.0	0.1		**Campan**
turn right on D8						
43° 01' 02.05" N	43.01724°	00°	10' 37.51" E			0.17709°
						663 meters
			46.1			parking, **Campan**

Col d'Aspin Details:

Distance—23.1 kilometers
Climbing—795 meters
Challenge rank—5.5
Parking: at the lot near D8 in Campan.

Bicycle southeast 6 kilometers through Campan to Ste-Marie-de-Campan. From the left turn in Ste-Marie-de-Campan climb 12½ kilometers to the summit. From the summit, retrace the route back to Campan.

There is one climb on the route. It starts at the parking lot in Campan and steeply climbs 829 meters in 18.6 kilometers with 5% to 12% ascents.

Col d'Aspin

From Ste-Marie-de-Campan, the ascent is 12.8 kilometers in length, ascending 642 meters, at an average 5% grade. In comparison with the Col du Tourmalet, this is considered a less difficult climb, with only the last five kilometers, at about 8% ascent, being difficult.

Summit

The pass has been part of the Tour de France 71 times, largely because it is the middle link in a chain of three road climbs, the other links being the Col du Tourmalet and Col de Peyresourde. The first time the Col d'Aspin was crossed was in 1910, when the leader over the summit was Octave Lapize.

Pyrénées Peaks

In the 1950 Tour, there was an altercation at the pass, with bottles and stones being thrown at the riders. The Italian team with Gino Bartali and Fiorenzo Magni, the leaders at the time, withdrew from the Tour at the end of the stage from Pau to St-Gaudens.

(Continued on page 104)

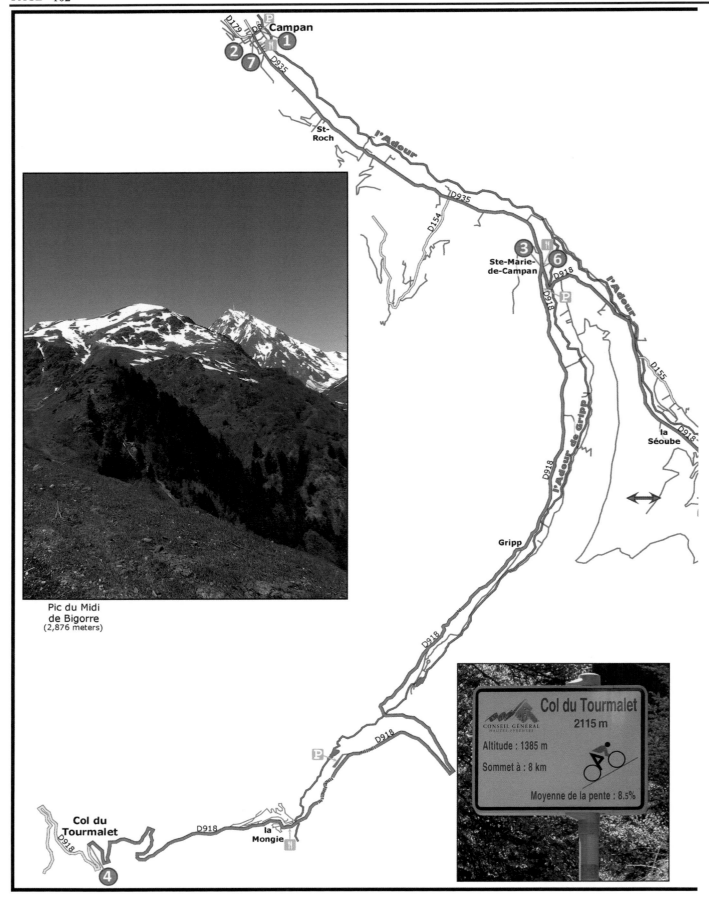

D179

D8

Campan
①

②

⑦

D935

St-Roch

l'Adour

D935

D154

③ ⑥
Ste-Marie-de-Campan
D918

l'Adour

D155

la Séoube

D918

D918

l'Adour de Gripp

Gripp

D918

Pic du Midi
de Bigorre
(2,876 meters)

Col du Tourmalet
2115 m

CONSEIL GÉNÉRAL
HAUTES-PYRÉNÉES

Altitude : 1385 m

Sommet à : 8 km

Moyenne de la pente : 8.5%

D918

Col du Tourmalet

D918

D918

la Mongie

④

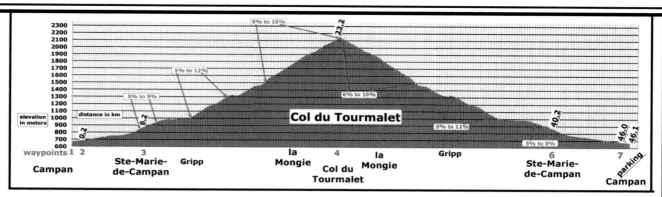

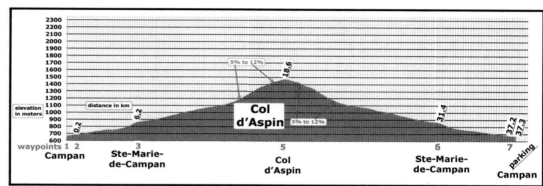

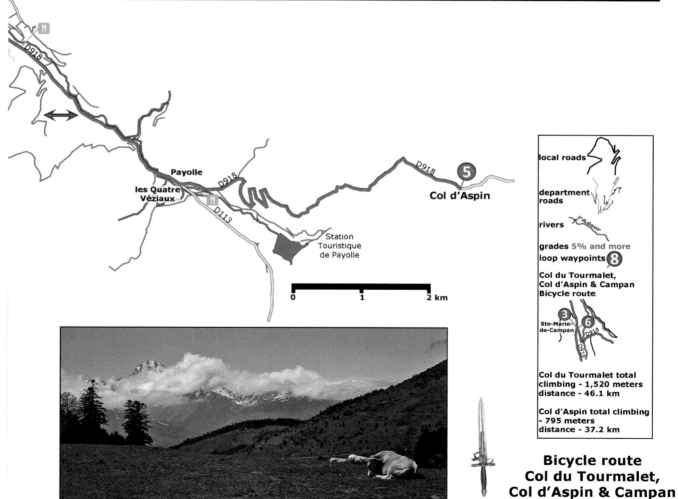

local roads

department roads

rivers

grades 5% and more

loop waypoints 8

Col du Tourmalet, Col d'Aspin & Campan Bicycle route

Ste-Marie-de-Campan

Col du Tourmalet total climbing - 1,520 meters
distance - 46.1 km

Col d'Aspin total climbing - 795 meters
distance - 37.2 km

**Bicycle route
Col du Tourmalet,
Col d'Aspin & Campan**

Col d'Aspin Waypoints

Queues and Directions

Segment	Waypoint		Km at start of segment	Km in segment	
①	↑ W	D8	0.0	0.2	**Campan**
depart W on D8					
43° 01' 03.93" N	43.01776°	00°	42' 10.48" E		0.70541°
829 meter ascent in 18.6 km					659 meters
②	◄⌐ SE	D935	0.2	6.0	**Campan**
turn left on D935					**St-Roch** at 1.8 km
D154 on right at 4.2 km					5% to 9% ascents
③	◄⌐ N	D918	6.2	12.4	**Ste-Marie-de-Campan**
turn left on D918					
42° 59' 04.68" N	42.98463°	00°	13' 39.00" E		0.22750°
D113 on right at 13.2 km				5% to 12% ascents	861 meters
⑤	⍐NW	D918	18.6	12.8	**Col d'Aspin**
U-turn on D918					
42° 54' 29.57" N	42.90821°	00°	08' 42.28" E		0.14508°
D113 on left at 25.6 km				5% to 12% descents	1,488 meters
⑥	S	D935	31.4	5.8	**Ste-Marie-de-Campan**
turn left on D935					5% to 9% descents
42° 59' 04.68" N	42.98463°	00°	13' 39.00" E		0.22750°
D154 on left at 33.4 km				**St-Roch** at 35.6 km	861 meters
⑦	⌐► E	D8	37.2	0.1	**Campan**
turn right on D8					
43° 01' 02.05" N	43.01724°	00°	10' 37.51" E		0.17709°
					663 meters
			37.3		parking, **Campan**

Col du Tourmalet Approach

Col d'Aspin Bulls

Campan War Memorial

Campan Market

Resources & Contacts

Area Interest

Bordeaux
   http://www.bordeaux.org.uk

Canal de Garonne
   http://canaldegaronne2.com/

The Pyrénées-Atlantiques
   http://www.princeton.edu/~achaney/tmve/wiki100k/docs/
   Pyrénées-Atlantiques.html

Bordeaux Cozy B&B
   http://www.chambredhotebordeaux.com/indexUS.html

Gite near Buxet-sur-Baïse
   http://www.domaine-de-baiise.com/

South of Pau near the Pyrénées, la Vignotte
   http://www.gites-de-france-64.com/la-vignotte/

Hotel booking service with descriptions and ratings
   http://hotels.france-bookings.com/index.html

Fiction of interest
   Eleanor of Aquitaine and the Four Kings by Amy Kelly
   ISBN 0-674-24254-8

Bicycling

Bicycle rental near Bordeaux (delivery around Bordeaux included)
   http://www.o2cycles.com/Pages/default.aspx
Bicycle rental, Aquitaine
   http://www.freewheelingfrance.com/bike-hire-in-france/bike-
   hire-in-aquitaine.html

Transportation in France

RailEurope, 9501 W. Devon Avenue, Suite 301, Rosemont, IL
60018 800-782-2424
   www.raileurope.com/us/index.htm

Automobile rental
   www.europcar.com

Acknowledgements

I am still grateful to my family for their curiosity about various cultures and their customs; to my brother and brother-in-law for an interest in cartography. My mother instilled knowledge of the English language starting in my early years, but not always infusing wisdom.

Local friends, neighbors and bicycling enthusiasts often helped with constructive comments on writing, bicycling and graphic presentation.

My thanks to Ed Merewether and Will Carleton for their inspiration and support.

My physicians, Carlos Govantes and C. A. Toumbis, always supportive, were extra helpful with added backbone this year.

Barbara Cabrera, for the tenth time, took on the challenging mission of editing this book. She accomplished this with diplomacy, dispatch and attention to detail of both French and English. I cannot gauge, nor adequately remunerate, her dedication to my writing.

Finally, I could not have completed *Bordeaux & the Pyrénées: A Bicycling Your France Guidebook* without my wife Shirley's unstinting encouragement of this vocation, her detailed reading and rereading of the manuscript, continued timely and significant comments, love and friendship.

I am fortunate to have received the above excellent help and guidance. Any errors of fact, language and consistency are mine alone.